PRAISE FOR
The Monk Who Sold His Ferrari

"Nothing less than sensational. This book will bless your life." Mark Victor Hansen, co-author, *Chicken Soup for the Soul*

"A captivating story that teaches as it delights." Paulo Coelho, author of *The Alchemist*

"This is a fun, fascinating, fanciful adventure into the realms of personal development, personal effectiveness and individual happiness. It contains treasures of wisdom that can enrich and enhance the life of every single person." Brian Tracy, author of *Maximum Achievement*

"Robin S. Sharma has an important message for all of us—one that can change our lives. He's written a one-of-a-kind handbook for personal fulfillment in a hectic age." Scott DeGarmo, past publisher, *Success Magazine*

"Robin Sharma has created an enchanting tale that incorporates the classic tools of transformation into a simple philosophy of living. A delightful book that will change your life." Elaine St. James, author of *Simplify Your Life* and *Inner Simplicity*

"... sheds light on life's big questions." *The Edmonton Journal*

"The Monk Who Sold His Ferrari is coherent, useful and definitely worth reading... It can truly help readers cope with the rat race." *The Kingston Whig-Standard*

"A magnificent book. Robin S. Sharma is the next Og Mandino." Dottie Walters, author of *Speak & Grow Rich*

"... simple wisdom that anyone can benefit from." *The Calgary Herald*

"This book could be classified as *The Wealthy Barber* of personal development... [It contains] insightful messages on the key concepts which help bring greater balance, control and effectiveness in our daily lives." *Investment Executive*

"... a treasure—an elegant and powerful formula for true success and happiness. Robin S. Sharma has captured the wisdom of the ages and made it relevant for these turbulent times. I couldn't put it down." Joe Tye, author of *Never Fear, Never Quit*

"... simple rules for reaching one's potential." *The Halifax Daily News*
"A wonderful story sharing lessons that can enrich your life." Ken Vegotsky, author of *The Ultimate Power*

"Sharma guides readers toward enlightenment." *The Chronicle-Herald*

"A wonderfully crafted parable revealing a set of simple yet surprisingly potent ideas for improving the quality of anyone's life. I'm recommending this gem of a book to all of my clients." George Williams, president, Karat Consulting International

"Robin Sharma offers personal fulfillment along the spiritual highroad." *The Ottawa Citizen*

PRAISE FOR
Leadership Wisdom from The Monk Who Sold His Ferrari

"One of the Year's Best Business Books." *PROFIT Magazine*

"... very informative, easy to read and extremely helpful.... We have distributed copies to all our management team as well as to store operators. The feedback has been very positive." David Bloom, CEO, Shoppers Drug Mart

"Robin Sharma has a neat, down-to-earth way of expressing his powerful solutions for today's most pressing leadership issues. This is so refreshing in a period when businesspeople are faced with so much jargon." Ian Turner, manager, Celestica Learning Centre

"This book is a gold mine of wisdom and common sense." Dean Larry Tapp, Richard Ivey School of Business, University of Western Ontario

"A terrific book that will help any businessperson lead and live more effectively." Jim O'Neill, director of operations, District Sales Division, London Life

"Monk points the way to balance in business... the books work ..." *The Toronto Star*

"*Leadership Wisdom from The Monk Who Sold His Ferrari* is headed for a top spot on the bestseller list." *Investment Executive*

"Sharma's mission is to provide the reader with insight to become a visionary leader, helping them transform their business into an organization that thrives in this era of change." *Sales Promotion Magazine*

"Sharma combines the wisdom of the great philosophers from the West and the East and applies it to the business world." *The Liberal*

"Sharma uses lessons from past masters to shed light on how we can handle the tensions of a high-tech, fast-changing world." *The Red Deer Advocate*

FAMILY WISDOM

from

THE MONK
WHO SOLD HIS FERRARI

Also by Robin Sharma

The Saint, the Surfer, and the CEO
The Monk Who Sold His Ferrari
Leadership Wisdom from The Monk Who Sold His Ferrari

For more information on Robin Sharma's books,
audio programs, videos, and learning tools, please visit:
www.robinsharma.com and **www.hayhouse.com**

FAMILY WISDOM

from

THE MONK WHO SOLD HIS FERRARI

Nurturing the Leader Within Your Child

Robin Sharma

HAY HOUSE, INC.
Carlsbad, California
London • Sydney • Johannesburg
Vancouver • Hong Kong

Published and distributed in the United States by: Hay House, Inc.,
P.O. Box 5100, Carlsbad, CA 92018-5100 • *Phone:* (760) 431-7695 or (800)
654-5126 • *Fax:* (760) 431-6948 or (800) 650-5115 • www.hayhouse.com •
Published and distributed in Australia by: Hay House Australia Ltd.,
18/36 Ralph St., Alexandria NSW 2015 • *Phone:* 612-9669-4299 •
Fax: 612-9669-4144 • www.hayhouse.com.au • **Published and distributed
in the United Kingdom by:** Hay House UK, Ltd. • Unit 202, Canalot Studios •
222 Kensal Rd., London W10 5BN • *Phone:* 44-20-8962-1230 •
Fax: 44-20-8962-1239 • www.hayhouse.co.uk • **Published and distributed
in the Republic of South Africa by:** Hay House SA (Pty), Ltd., P.O. Box
990, Witkoppen 2068 • *Phone/Fax:* 2711-7012233 • orders@psdprom.co.za

Originally published by Harper Collins Publishers Ltd, Toronto Canada.
Copyright © 2000 • ISBN: 0-00-200039-3

Library of Congress Cataloging-in-Publication Data

Sharma, Robin.
  Family wisdom from the monk who sold his Ferrari : nurturing the
leader within your child / Robin Sharma.
     p. cm.
  ISBN 1-40190-014-3 (tradepaper)
  1. Parenting. 2. Conduct of life. 3. Family life. 4. Child
rearing. I. Title.
  HQ769 .S4856 2003
  649'.1—dc21
                              2002011521

ISBN 1-4019-0014-3

06 05 04 03   5 4 3 2
1st Hay House printing, September 2003
2nd Hay House printing, September 2003

Printed in the United States of America

I dedicate this book to my extraordinary children, Colby and Bianca, two of the greatest and wisest teachers in my life. I love you both very very much.

I also dedicate this book to my dear friend and colleague, the late George Williams, a man who touched many lives but left us far too early.

Finally, I dedicate this book to you, the reader. May the lessons you discover on these pages inspire you to be a wiser person, a better parent, and to become the kind of family leader who will inspire the children of the world to live bigger and better lives.

❧

*"A hundred years from now it will not matter
what my bank account was, the sort of house
I lived in or the kind of car I drove. But
the world may be different because I was
important in the life of a child."*
—Author unknown

"To live in hearts we leave behind is not to die."
—Thomas Campbell

Contents

Acknowledgments

FIRST I MUST THANK ALL THE PEOPLE around the world who have read the books in *The Monk Who Sold His Ferrari* series, as well those who have helped *The Saint, The Surfer, and The CEO* become a word-of-mouth phenomenon. I feel so very blessed to be able to share my reflections on what it means to live an authentic and beautiful life with you.

Thanks must also go to my wonderful team at Sharma Leadership International who help me advance my mission of helping people discover who they truly are and live their best lives in the process. I gratefully acknowledge Al Moscardelli, Marnie Ballane, and Marie Witten for the dedication to our "crusade" to make a difference in the world.

Appreciation must also go to our much-valued clients for inviting me into your organizations as a leadership speaker, coach, and consultant. It has been a joy to add value and help you create workplaces where it's safe to be human again. I also specifically thank members of our *Monthly Coach* program for having the courage to keep playing your highest game as you advance in your lives, as well as my *Masters Series* coaching clients for playing as leaders on the planet.

To my agent, Ken Browning, you are a superstar and gifted at what you do. Thank you for your faith in me. And huge thanks to the incredible team at Hay House in California. Jill Kramer, my editor; Danny Levin; Reid Tracy; and Chandra Teitscheid have been so helpful in spreading my message and in making my experience as an author a genuine joy.

As always, I express appreciation to my colleagues John Gray, Mark Victor Hansen, Denis Waitley, Wayne Dyer, Nido Qubein, and to my friends Jeffrey Feldberg, Gerry Weiner, Darren Bagshaw, Dan Sheehan, Azim Jamal, Richard Carlson, and Ed Carson for the contributions you have made to my life.

I thank my amazing brother, Sanjay; his wonderful wife, Susan; and my parents, Shiv and Shashi, who have done so much for me in so many ways. Finally, I express my gratitude to my two incredible children, Colby and Bianca, for being the greatest examples in my life of unconditional and true love.

Introduction

THIS IS A WORK OF FICTION. It's the story of a raven-ously ambitious woman named Catherine Cruz who sacrificed her family life and the things that were truly important to her for the call of fast-lane success. However, as so often happens when we walk down the inauthentic path of life, she reached a crisis point that caused her to go deep and rethink the way that she thought, felt, and lived. What she discovered trans-formed not only her family life but her inner world as well. And the remarkable guide who led her through this extraordinary transformation will transform your life, too.

While the characters in this modern-day fable about creating an extraordinary family life are from my imagination, the philosophies, lessons, and tools articulated in this book are *very* real. The *5 Masteries of the Family Leader* have helped tens of thousands of parents bring deep love into their family cultures and re-create their home lives. In the process, these individuals have also reconnected to their best selves and brought a profound sense of balance into their world. Many of the ideas that you'll read on the pages that follow come from my personal experience as the father of two young children. The primary priority of my life is to inspire and nurture my children to grow into their most authentic selves and show up as leaders as they mature along the journey of life.

As parents, we only have a small window of opportunity to influence the lives of our children and to be the model of unconditional love in their lives. Children grow up so very quickly, and it's easy, in the fast-paced world we live in, to promise ourselves that we'll deeply connect with them "when things slow down" or "next month when I have a little more time" or "once things at work become a little more certain." But the weeks slip into months, and the months slip into years, and before you know it your children are off living lives of their own. The wise philosopher Kahlil Gibran, in his beautiful book *The Prophet,* writes: "Your children are not your children. They are the sons and daughters of Life's longing for itself." I could not agree more. A time will eventually come when you have to give your children back to life. It is my deep hope that *Family Wisdom from the Monk Who Sold His Ferrari* will inspire and assist you as you create a beautiful family life and help your children grow into the leaders that they've always been meant to be.

One final note: If you really want to "own this material," it's very important that you teach it. I suggest that within 24 hours of completing this book, you sit down and share the philosophies and ideas that you've learned with a family member. This will clarify and deepen your understanding of the material and bring its lessons strongly into your life. I also invite you to connect with others in our community of individuals dedicated to bringing more love, understanding, and leadership into this uncertain world. To do so, simply visit **robinsharma.com** and begin to engage in conversations with other like-minded parents and individuals walking the path to their highest and best selves.

— **Robin Sharma**

My Great Awakening

"We are generally afraid to become that which we can glimpse in our most perfect moments."
—Abraham Maslow

THE SADDEST PART OF LIFE lies not in the act of dying, but in failing to truly live while we are alive. Too many of us play small with our lives, never letting the fullness of our humanity see the light of day. I've learned that what really counts in life, in the end, is not how many toys we've collected or how much money we've accumulated, but how many of our talents we've liberated and used for a purpose that adds value to this world. What truly matters most are the lives we've touched and the legacy that we've left. Tolstoy put it so well when he wrote: "We live for ourselves only when we live for others."

My name is Catherine Cruz, and it took me forty years to discover this simple point of wisdom. Forty long years to discover that success cannot really be pursued. Success *ensues* and flows into your life as the unintended yet inevitable by-product of a life spent enriching the lives of other people. When you shift your daily focus from a compulsion to survive to a lifelong commitment to serve, your existence cannot help but explode into success.

I still can't believe that I had to wait until the "halftime" of my life to figure out that true fulfillment as a human being comes not from achieving those grand gestures that put us on the front pages of the newspapers and business magazines, but instead from those basic and incremental acts of decency that each one of us has the privilege to practice each and every day if we simply make the choice to do so. Mother Teresa, a great leader of human hearts if ever there was one, said it best: "There are no great acts, only small acts done with great love." I learned this the hard way in my life.

Until recently, I had been so busy striving, that I'd missed out on living. I was so busy chasing life's big pleasures that I'd missed out on the little ones, those micro-joys that weave themselves in and out of our lives on a daily basis but often go unnoticed. My days were over-scheduled, my mind was overworked, and my spirit was underfed. To be honest with you, my life reflected outward success but was completely bankrupt in terms of inner significance.

I was of the old school that believed that happiness would arrive when I bought the right car, built the right house, and was promoted to the right job. I judged the value of a human being not by the size of their heart and the strength of their character, but by the size of their wallet and the contents of their bank account. You might say that I was not a good person. I would argue that I simply had no idea about the true meaning of life or how to conduct myself as I lived it. Maybe it was the kind of people I associated with, but everyone I knew in the business world lived by this same philosophy. We all dedicated the best hours of our days to climbing the stairway of success that we dreamed would lead us into the coveted corner office, the opulent summer home in the Hamptons, and perhaps that spectacular ski chalet in France. We all wanted to be famous, admired, and honored. We all wanted to be filthy rich. And, most of all, we all wanted to be wanted.

And though I did entertain the idea of being a mother one day and raising a family in the future, the dreams of my quietest moments were more along the lines of appearing on the cover of *Forbes* or *Fortune* magazine with the headline under my sleek figure stating: "Catherine Cruz: the CEO Who Broke All the Rules and Still Won," than cheering on children at little league games. On the way to work, I used to repeat affirmations like "Today will be the best day of my life" and "I have the millionaire's mind and the warrior's heart." I can just see you shaking your head right now, but I wanted success so badly back then I would have done anything for it. I would have said whatever people asked me to say, done whatever anyone told me to do, and climbed over anyone who had the misfortune to get in my way. I'm not saying I'm proud of the person I was back then. I'm just telling you that that's who I was. I was tough, ruthless, ambitious, and driven—to a fault, closing down my emotional side in an effort to survive in the world I had made for myself.

My life was defined by my work, and I felt I was destined to reach the pinnacle of success in business. On my office wall were these words of the great English poet Henry Wadsworth Longfellow that I believed said it all:

> *Lives of great men all remind us*
> *We can make our lives sublime,*
> *And, departing, leave behind us*
> *Footprints on the sands of time.*

Sure, my pals from grad school and I learned to pay lip service to all those honey-covered platitudes such as "People come first" and "People don't care how much you know until they know how much you care" that were served up all too frequently by well-heeled consultants and well-meaning business professors. But deep within each one of us, there lived only one desire: to serve ourselves and meet our own goals, hopes, and dreams—

no matter how many people we had to trample to do it. And so we sacrificed our very souls for the sake of professional success and the pursuit of big money. We gave everything we had to our work. And though I'm now embarrassed to admit it, in the early years it was fun. Really fun.

As the brightest student in my class, I had my pick of the best companies on the planet to work for. Having always been a bit of a rebel, I delighted in rejecting every one of their six-figure offers, much to the chagrin of my mother, who thought I was out of my mind. Remembering the advice of one of my favorite professors in business school, himself a person who chose to walk the road less traveled (he preached: "When searching for your ideal job, stop asking 'Is this a company I'd like to work for?' and start asking 'Is this a company that I'd like to own?'"), I settled on a fast-track management position with a little-known financial services firm with massive growth potential. Never discount the power of stock options to attract even the most uninterested job candidate.

Every morning at precisely 5:15, my shiny black Mercedes—a signing bonus from my new employer— sped through the underground parking lot of the seventy-story glass-and-metal office tower that I was to spend the next few years of my life within. With a fresh copy of *The Wall Street Journal* in one hand and my alligator skin attaché case in the other, I strode to the bank of elevators and then up to the sixty-second floor office. This was my real home.

Once there, I would check my messages, return all phone calls, and then proceed to live out the next sixteen to eighteen hours in a state of high anxiety and near chaos. In short order, I was promoted to divisional, and then senior, vice-president, all before I was thirty-five. I had the pleasure of flying around the world first-class, rubbing shoulders with the business elite, eating in the finest restaurants, and doing deals that would make my contemporaries shudder with jealousy. I was eventually given a luxurious office, and I finally did buy that ski chalet, thanks to my stock options that, as I had hoped, soared through the stratosphere.

A few years ago, a few friends from business school and I started a Web-based company we called BraveLife.com that provided corporations with a revolutionary new way to train and develop employees wishing to excel in these wildly competitive times. Although it was initially something we did just for fun, BraveLife.com became an instant hit, and within months, our unique enterprise was featured in just about every major business publication in the nation. With the pundits saying this venture was an ideal candidate for a public offering, and venture capitalists hovering around us like vultures closing in for the kill, my partners and I knew we would soon be rich. It was all coming together, just as I had envisioned in so many of my quieter moments. I would be wealthy, celebrated, and beloved. I could afford all the material possessions I craved so deeply, and finally have the resources to live my life on my own terms. I was well on my way to the mountaintop and living the life I had always wanted. And yet, as I drew closer to my dreams, I stumbled upon a strange realization that took the wind out of my sails. No matter what I tried to do to deny it, I was a completely miserable human being.

I was seven years into a marriage that lacked any trace of passion or emotional connection. I met my husband, Jon Cruz, at a wilderness retreat the company I initially worked for had sent its high-performing executives to in order to refine our leadership skills. Jon was a struggling entrepreneur hoping to find some inspiration in the mountains, and we found ourselves on the same team, faced with the mission of scaling a challenging rock face in the middle of the night. He admired my fearlessness and tenacity, and I was immediately attracted to his gentleness and passion for life. We fell in love, and though it ran contrary to my cautious ways, we were married six weeks later.

Jon was a good man in a world where raw goodness and strength of character are no longer given the value they deserve. Our early years together saw lots of good times, but as the years progressed, our relationship started to fall apart through the process of neglect. He loved nature and the great outdoors, and I loved glitzy restaurants and highbrow fashion shows. He collected great books and enjoyed carving wood on the backyard patio, while I collected great wines and appreciated fine art. But I must tell you that it was not our differences that led to our less-than-ideal marriage. The real problem was that I was never home with my husband.

By the time I'd roll into the driveway at night, Jon would be asleep. And by the time he'd get up, my Mercedes would be winding its way to my office. Although we lived under one roof, it would be safe to say we lived separate lives. But it was far more than my relationship with Jon that was causing me to feel so empty and disheartened as a person. We had two young—and wonderful—children I knew were suffering as a result of my eternal absences. They did not say a word to me about all the time I spent at the office, but their eyes revealed the fulness of their disappointment and their deep need to have a richer connection with the woman they called Mom.

Porter, our son, was just turning six; and Sarita, our daughter, was three. I knew that these early years were by far the most important in terms of the shaping and development of their characters. I knew that this was the stage during which they needed to be surrounded by great, loving role models who lavished affection and wisdom upon their tender souls. I knew that I would regret the many hours I spent away from them, but for some inexplicable reason, I just could not tear myself away from my office and all the obligations my hyper-complex professional life carried with it.

"Life is nothing more than a series of windows of opportunity strung together to form a whole," my wise father used to tell me. I had the common sense and intelligence to appreciate that Porter and Sarita would only be young once, and that now was the time that they needed my presence. Once this window of opportunity closed, my chance to equip them with the values, virtues, and vision to lead rich lives as they matured would be gone forever. And I knew I could never forgive myself for not being there for them when they needed me most. I guess I just didn't have the courage to step back from my chaotic life and really reflect on my highest priorities, nor the wisdom to ensure that these priorities were reflected in the way I spent my days. No matter how hard I tried, I just couldn't bring myself to stop working at a blistering pace and restore balance in my life. I truly felt that I could not live without the adrenaline rush and sense of significance my overflowing agenda gave me. As much as I'd publicly profess that my family was what truly counted, the facts clearly revealed otherwise. All the evidence showed that Jon and the kids finished a distant second to my career and my desire to become rich.

The Best
Worst Experience
of My Life

*"If I had to live my life over again, I would
relax more. I'd be sillier than I have been on
this trip. I would climb more mountains, swim
more rivers, and watch more sunsets. I would
have more actual troubles and less imaginary
ones. Oh, I've had my moments, and if I had to
do it over again, I'd have more of them. In fact,
I'd try to have nothing else, just moments, one
after another. And I'd pick more daisies."*
—Nadine Stair, age 89

MOST PEOPLE DON'T REALLY DISCOVER what life is all about until they come to die. Then, facing their mortality head on, they awaken to life's deepest meanings and realize all that they have missed. Life can be cruel in that way. Its gifts all too often fail to appear until the very end. When we are young and have our whole lives ahead of us, we tend to put off living. "Next year I'll spend more time in nature or laugh more or love more. Next year I'll spend more time with my kids and read the great works of literature. Next year I will watch more sunsets and build better friendships. But right now, I've got things to do and people to meet." These are the standard refrains of the age we live in.

Well, I've learned that if you don't act on life, life has a habit of acting on you. And the days slip into weeks, and the weeks into months, and before you know it, your life will be over. The point of wisdom is clear: *stop living your life by default and start living your life by design.* Get back into the game, and take action to create the richer reality you know deep within your heart you were destined to create. Today, begin to live your life the way you will wish you had lived when you lay on your deathbed. Or, to paraphrase Mark Twain, live out your life in such a way that even the undertaker cries at your funeral.

It's a strange world we live in. We can send a missile across the world with pinpoint accuracy, yet we have trouble walking across the street to meet a new neighbor. We spend more time watching television than we do connecting with our children. We say we want to change the world but are not willing to change ourselves. Then, as the sun sets on our lives and we allow ourselves some time for a little deep reflection, we catch a glimpse of the joys we could have experienced, the kindnesses we could have given, and the people we could have been. But by then, it's too late. By the time most of us wake up to living, it's time to lie down. Thankfully, my awakening came sooner.

I was headed to San Francisco to speak at a high-tech conference about the success of BraveLife.com. I had almost missed my flight due to a major snowstorm that had paralyzed most of the city and ground traffic to a halt. After finally boarding the plane, my two business partners and I had settled into our first-class seats with an exceptionally good glass of wine and a discussion about how we would handle the presentation we had been asked to make. We chatted for about thirty minutes, and then, feeling exhausted after a full day at the office, I excused myself from the discussion and drifted off to sleep.

Suddenly, I was awakened by the captain's voice over the public address system. "We are experiencing some really choppy weather up here, folks. And it looks like it's going to get even rougher. Please be sure that your seatbelt is fastened snugly around your waist, and place your tray table in the upright position," came the familiar instruction. Although he tried his best to sound calm, the captain's voice betrayed him, and I wondered if there was something far more serious he was dealing with. My heart began to pound as he continued to speak. "It looks like all this inclement weather has created some real challenges for us up here on the flight deck. Again, please keep your seatbelts fastened, and I'll keep you updated about this storm we are heading into as soon as we know more."

The next thing I knew, the cabin lights went out and the emergency lighting system came on. The plane started shaking violently, and plates started falling to the floor. The turbulence, which had initially been bearable, soon became too much to take and made me sick to my stomach. I looked at the face of my partner, Jack—he looked like a young Warren Beatty and had two young children at home, like myself. Normally a master of grace under pressure, he was clearly horrified by what was happening and started to hyperventilate. As he shakily grabbed my hand, he forced out eight words I will never forget: "Catherine, I think we are going to crash."

It's hard for me to describe to you how I felt during the next few minutes. I knew that Jack was right, but oddly, a strange sense of peace and acceptance came over me. Clutching his hand tightly, I closed my eyes. And I thought about my children. My heart sank as an image of Porter's smiling face danced across the picture screen of my mind. I remembered his first words and this great little boy's first steps. I saw him laughing in the tree-house Jon had built for him in our backyard, munching on a carrot dipped in peanut butter, a snack he told us would make him into a superhero when he grew older. I saw a giggling Sarita jumping up and down on her bed and singing nursery rhymes at the top of her lungs. And then I saw Jon relaxing on the back porch next to the barbeque he joked he loved more than me, sipping on an ice-cold Corona with a wedge of lime tucked over the top.

Almost in slow motion, I then saw all four of us on the only vacation we ever took as a family: we had gone up to Canada and traveled through the Rockies. Here's the interesting thing, though—of all those hundreds of thoughts that I had in those last few moments before the plane crashed, not a single one was about myself or my business. I guess it's true what the wisest among us have said for centuries: *at the end of your life you will find that the things you thought were the big things were actually the little things, and that all those things you thought were the little, unimportant things were actually the big, important ones.*

At that low moment of my life, staring death in the face, I did not think about the money I made or the car I drove or the title inscribed on my business card. My thoughts did not drift to the profit our company had made or the magazine covers I had been featured on. *All I could think about was my family.* And how much I loved them, how much I would miss them, and how deeply I regretted not devoting more time to them. My dad used to say that he had never seen a U-Haul following a hearse on the way to a funeral. His point, undoubtedly, was that no matter how many things you collect over the course of your lifetime, you cannot take them with you. The only thing we can take with us is our memories, memories of The Things That Truly Count. Facing my mortality head on, I came to the ultimate realization: my family mattered most.

The Gift of Life

"To believe in the heroic makes heroes."
—Benjamin Disraeli

THE NEXT THING I REMEMBER was waking up as I was being rushed into an emergency room by a team of screaming paramedics. I drifted in and out of consciousness for the next few minutes and heard someone yell: "We're losing her. Losing all vital signs. Get this woman onto the operating table stat!"

My God, I thought, *I've just survived a plane crash.* My clothes were soaked in blood, and gaping wounds riddled my arms and legs. I felt cold and disoriented. And I was thirsty; I've never been so thirsty in all my life. Then I realized that I just might die on the operating table.

I had no idea what city I was in. I didn't know if my family had been informed of the tragedy. I didn't know if my two partners were alive. But soon my fear turned to calm, and for some reason, I knew I would live. I've since learned that the universe unfolds as it should and that everything that happens to us in life happens for a reason. Our setbacks inevitably carry blessings and bring with them lessons that we need to learn in order to move to the next level of living. The great English poet Henry Wadsworth Longfellow expressed the point so well when he observed, "It has done me good to be some-what parched by the heat and drenched by the rain of life." I knew I had survived this tragic accident for some reason. I just couldn't figure out what that reason was. And I had no idea what my lesson would be.

After spending nearly twelve hours in the operating room, I was shipped off to the critical-care ward to begin the grueling process of recovery. The next morning, I was awakened by the two sweetest sounds my ears have ever heard—Porter's and Sarita's voices. "Mommy, wake up. Mommy, wake up! We love you," they repeated in mantra-like fashion. When I finally managed to open my eyes, I saw Porter there in his favorite Curious George T-shirt, and Sarita in the little red overalls she insisted on wearing most of the time. Jon was standing with them, tears streaming down his cheeks, unable to speak even a word. Then they hugged me. And we all began to cry.

I spent months in that hospital bed. Sadly, the plane crash had claimed many lives, including those of Jack and Ross, my business partners—a loss that devastated me. The three of us had experienced so much together over the previous few years, and I had no interest in running the company without them. They were not simply the co-founders of Bravelife.com; Jack and Ross had become my best friends. The final cause of the accident, according to the FAA, was determined to be "pilot error," and as the lawyers stepped in to make their claims, I vowed to put this event behind me and do whatever I needed to do to get back on my feet and return to my family. Although Jon and the kids visited me every day, I spent most of my time in rehabilitation, making an effort to speed up the healing process. The doctors and nurses at the hospital were like angels sent from above, showering me with attention, kindness, and compassion. As the days passed, I grew stronger and my future began to look brighter. But then one night, something extremely strange happened to me.

Visiting hours had just ended and Jon had taken the children home for the night. I had just started reading a wonderful book called *Hope for the Flowers* by Trina Paulus, which I was finding to be not only inspirational but also deeply enlightening. As I reached for the cup of hot tea on my bedside table, I saw someone in an electric wheelchair whisk by the doorway to my room at an alarming rate.

I was surprised that someone would be moving so quickly in a hospital at such a late hour, but decided to turn my attention back to my reading. I had given up this important habit when the demands of work became all-consuming, but ever since the plane crash I had vowed to get back to The Things That Truly Count. Reading something from the wisdom literature every day was one of those things. The crash had been an epiphany for me, the wake-up call I needed to rethink my priorities and clean up my life. In the solitude of my hospital room, I did some deep thinking, and reflected, for the first time in many years, on the way I had been conducting myself—as a parent, as a partner, and as a human being. I felt that I had been given a second chance to live—this time around, I would live with greater wisdom, decency, and virtue. I decided that I would get back to the fundamentals of great living and simplify my life.

"The best things are nearest: breath in your nostrils, light in your eyes, flowers at your feet, duties at your hand, the path of Right just before you. Do not grasp at the stars, but do life's plain common work as it comes, certain that daily duties and daily bread are the sweetest things in life," wrote Robert Louis Stevenson.

Just when I had focused on my book, it happened again. The figure in the wheelchair raced by my room a second time—but now he was going even faster. Even more surprisingly, this person was now singing at the top of his lungs. I recognized the song—I hadn't heard it in years. My parents used to sing it to me when I was a little girl, and I was surprised that this odd visitor knew the words. I had to find out who this person was. But would this be a safe thing to do? What if he were some crazed lunatic who had come in off the streets? Still, my curiosity got the better of me, and I rolled out of bed and grabbed my trusted walker.

I slowly went out into the hallway hoping to see who this maniac was. But I saw nothing. The hallway was completely empty, and totally silent except for two young nurses working at their station. "Oh, hello," I said warmly, as I made my way along the corridor.

"Hi, Catherine," they replied. "Everything okay?"

"Sure," I answered. "I was just wondering who that was flying down the hallway a few minutes ago. He was going far too fast for my liking. He could have hurt someone, you know. And why was he singing? If you see him again, please tell him to slow down. Tell him to get some singing lessons while you're at it," I said with a smile.

"We didn't see anyone," the nurses replied in unison.

"You didn't?" I asked in embarrassment.

"No, we didn't. Sorry, Catherine. Maybe you just had a bad dream."

"No, it wasn't a dream. I saw this strange-looking figure in one of those electric wheelchairs speeding down this hallway. And he was singing this children's song I used to love as a kid. I haven't heard that song for years."

I was beginning to realize how silly I sounded. The nurses started to laugh.

"You're pulling our legs, right?"

"No, I'm serious. If you see him again, talk to him," I said sternly. "He should act more responsibly."

"Okay, Catherine, we will," one of the nurses replied, still chuckling.

As I made my way back to my room, something on the floor caught my eye. The object was shiny and made of metal. As I turned it over and held it up to the light, I could not believe my eyes. It was a gold butterfly. I was astounded. My father had given a butterfly like this to me and to my older brother Julian to remind us to be free thinkers as we grew up and went on to lead lives of our own. To him, the butterfly was a symbol of freedom, independence, and beauty—qualities he hoped we would fill our lives with. He gave the gold butterflies to us on the day he was named a judge of the federal court. I remember feeling so very proud of my dad on that day. He had worked tirelessly to arrive at that position and deserved every bit of his success. Dad was such a good man: noble, loving, and honest to a fault.

I had kept my butterfly at home and treasured it as one of my most important belongings, especially after Dad died. I have no idea what my brother Julian did with his. Knowing Julian, he probably sold it. My brother was a unique character, I must tell you. You will probably never meet anyone quite like him in your life. I'm not sure how I would describe him to you. Yes, he was brilliant and talented and irreverent and wild. But he was so much more.

Growing up, he was always the smartest—and cockiest—kid in his class. Given his movie star looks, the prettiest girls in school always gravitated to him. Given his brains, he won every honor that the school had to bestow. In college, he was an elite athlete, a brilliant debater, a first-class student, and a world-class playboy. He just had these immense human gifts. It was far more than his intellect or his charisma. He had this amazing energy and light about him that was inescapable. And even more important, Julian had a good heart. I really loved him and saw him as my hero. We had such fun growing up, spending summers at our lakeside cottage and winters on the ski slope. Most of our time together was spent laughing and playing practical jokes on one another. Simply said, Julian was one amazing man. And I missed him deeply.

As expected, Julian graduated first in his class at Harvard Law School. He was the subject of an intense bidding war among the finest law firms in the country. In short order, he carved out a reputation as one of the best and brightest hired legal guns in the nation and achieved success that was impressive by any measure. Even my dad, a man who did not give praise lightly and who understood the true meaning of excellence, often remarked: "That boy really is good. Really good. I'd be willing to bet he'll be on the Supreme Court one day. A chip off the old block, I'd say," he would add with a laugh.

Julian's star shone brightly for many years. Respected as one of the smartest and toughest trial lawyers in the entire country, he earned an income in the seven figures and filled his life with the best that life had to offer. He purchased a spectacular mansion in a neighborhood favored by celebrities and ambassadors. He invested in a private jet to whisk him from client to client in royal style and would fly tailors in from Italy just to make him a suit for a big trial. He even bought a home on a private island that he named "Nirvana" in hopes that it would serve as a place of renewal where he might recover from the blistering pace he had chosen to keep. But of all Julian's possessions, the one that he loved most was the shiny red Ferrari that he always kept parked in the center of his driveway. That car was his joy, his passion, and his reward for all the sacrifices he knew he had made along the road to his fast but well-deserved success.

Along the path of Julian's meteoric rise in the legal profession, my brother married a wonderful woman, and this golden couple had a beautiful daughter they named Ally. She was an amazing little girl—unusually bright, always laughing, and constantly getting into mischief. I've yet to see a child as luminous and lovely as Ally. Having a daughter changed everything for Julian. Sure, he still did extremely well as a lawyer, and his skills in the courtroom remained as sharp as ever. Sure, he still had that competitive fire that burned deep in his belly and compelled him to reach for the stars. But his priorities seemed to change as the days went by. I saw that he was beginning to love the life of a family man. He began taking every Friday off to do nothing more than play with his daughter and take her on outings with his wife. I remember him being so very happy at that time of his life.

While Julian had always been handsome and fit, his face actually seemed to glow when he was with his family. His eyes sparkled when he would show up with Ally, and I knew this was a man who had found the inner peace we all crave in this world of hypercomplexity and infinite uncertainty. Julian was surrounded by love and had the world by the tail. But life has a way of setting us back when we least expect or deserve it. Often it is when we are at the top of our game that our greatest suffering begins. At such times, all that is dear to us can be ripped out from under us, leaving us sitting in the darkness and facing the abyss. It is in those most bleak of moments that we catch a glimpse of who we truly are. It is in those times of greatest pain that our true character is revealed. It is in those lowest periods of life that we are introduced to our finest strengths. And something soon happened to my dear brother Julian that introduced him to strengths he could never imagine he had.

One sun-soaked autumn afternoon, as he drove little Ally to her best friend's birthday party, Julian noticed that a car in the opposite lane was starting to swerve into his lane. At first he thought nothing of it, but he grew concerned, as the car not only remained in his lane, but started to accelerate directly toward the car he and Ally were riding in. What happened in the next few seconds changed Julian's life forever. The driver of the other car, drunk after a day of hard drinking with his buddies, lost control and smashed head on into Julian's car. Unbelievably, Julian escaped with no more than a few bruises. But sadly, little Ally was not so fortunate. She was fatally injured when her head struck the windshield at the moment of the crash, and she died in my brother's arms as he sat in the middle of the road screamimg for medical assistance. After this unspeakable loss, Julian was never the same. He was transformed from a man who lived every day to the fullest to a man who struggled to survive each passing hour. It broke my heart.

In a desperate attempt to avoid confronting his sorrow, he began spending every waking hour at work, sometimes spending weeks on end sleeping on the couch in his lavish office and refusing to meet with anyone who might remind him of the life he once knew. And while this tunnel vision led Julian to even greater success in his career, it created equally great decay on the personal front. Carlos Castaneda once wrote that "the basic difference between an ordinary man and a warrior is that a warrior takes everything as a challenge while the ordinary man takes everything as either a blessing or a curse." I think that Julian felt he was cursed.

His lovely wife eventually decided to leave him, saying that his obsession with work and his emotional unavailability made life with him unbearable. She confided in me that she'd done everything in her power to snap Julian out of the state he had fallen into, but nothing had worked. Even worse, he made it very clear from his words and actions that he was not open to receiving any help. Not from anyone. He just wanted to be left alone and wished everyone would "mind their own business and go shower their pity on someone else."

Julian began to drink excessively and live recklessly. He slept little, ate too much, and developed a rough exterior that pushed even those closest to him away. What little free time he had he would spend with impossibly thin fashion models or the rowdy band of stockbrokers he referred to as his "demolition team." Although I did not see much of Julian those days—he even refused to accept *my* phone calls—I knew he was headed for trouble. Deep trouble.

Once I spotted him rushing along a downtown street with two briefcases bulging with papers, sweat pouring off his forehead. His appearance that day brought tears to my eyes. I could not believe how my brother looked. His once youthful and handsome face had been replaced by a landscape of wrinkles, and his eyes spoke of deep sadness. The chiseled physique he was once so proud of had given way to a grossly overweight figure and a fallen posture. And the million-dollar smile that used to perpetually rest on his face had left without a trace. I felt so sad to see Julian, the brother whom I loved so much and had such admiration for, going through this private hell.

A few months later, I received a phone call from one of Julian's law partners. I was informed that my brother had suffered a massive heart attack in the middle of the courtroom while he was arguing a major civil case. He had been rushed to the hospital and, thankfully, would survive, the partner told me. But, as usual, Julian was refusing all visitors. "Especially family," his colleague emphasized.

"Couldn't I see him for even a few minutes?" I pleaded.

"I wish I could say yes, Catherine, but you know Julian. He has ordered everyone out of his room and instructed the hospital staff to keep the door closed at all times. He even threatened one of the senior doctors with a lawsuit if anyone was given access to the private telephone line they installed in his room for him."

That's so Julian, I thought. Even in his most vulnerable of moments, he was first and foremost a lawyer.

"There's something else I think you should know, Catherine," the partner added as his voice grew quieter. "I really can't believe this, but Julian has announced that he will give up the practice of law. He has tendered his resignation and is leaving the firm."

"You're kidding!" I exclaimed, scarcely able to believe what I was hearing. "The law is in Julian's blood, just like it was in Dad's. He's wanted to be a lawyer since he was five years old."

"I'm just telling you what he told me earlier today, Catherine," the partner replied in a tone that revealed his own shock at Julian's decision.

True to his word, within weeks Julian left the law. Even more astounding, within months he sold all his material possessions: the mansion, the plane, and the private island. He even sold his red Ferrari, the most obvious symbol of his success and of the man he once was. I learned through another one of his friends that Julian had retreated to India on some kind of "a search for life's deepest meaning," as his friend put it. Julian left no forwarding address, no phone number by which he could be contacted, and no indication as to when he would return.

"What's your guess?" I asked his friend.

"My guess is that neither you nor I will ever see the great Julian Mantle again," came the hushed reply.

As the years slipped by, I heard nothing from Julian, not even a postcard. It was as if he refused to acknowledge the existence of a sister or of the life he had before the death of his daughter. Failing to see that there were lessons to be learned from Julian's downfall, I too became consumed with my work, although I had started a family of my own. And even though I began to think less and less of Julian over time, in my quieter moments, often when Jon and the kids were asleep upstairs, I could not help wondering where my brother was and whether he was okay.

My mind would float back to those hot summer days when we'd swim off the dock at our summer place and sail our little boat along the lake. I'd recall Julian's sense of humor and the pranks he used to play on anyone who had the misfortune of causing him the slightest aggravation. And most of all, I remembered that mischievous sparkle that never left Julian's eyes. Through the miracle of genetics, Ally had acquired that same sparkle. My, how I missed that little girl. And my, how I longed to see my brother.

A Monk
Comes to Visit

"The happiness or unhappiness of a man does not depend upon the amount of property or gold he wins. Happiness or misery is in one's soul. A wise man feels at home in every country. The whole universe is the home of a noble soul."
—Democritus

"I'M YOUR NEW DOCTOR," boomed the voice from the darkened end of the hallway. As I looked up, I was astonished by what I saw. I watched a striking young man in a doctor's coat get up out of the wheelchair that had been flying down the corridor and begin to walk toward me from the darkness. And while he had the standard stethoscope hanging from his neck, something else that he was wearing took me by surprise. The young man appeared to be wearing a hooded red robe, the kind I've often seen Tibetan monks wear. It was elegantly cut and very beautiful in its texture, with intricate stitching along its flowing borders. While it was still difficult to see the man in the dim light, as he moved closer to me I sensed a remarkably youthful and handsome face that radiated a positive vitality and energy. I was also struck by how familiar this man looked.

Attired in sandals, with little flowers carved on them, the young man looked fit and strong and conveyed a special sense of confidence as well as inner peace. And his eyes, which I soon was able to see more clearly, looked like two sparkling diamonds—they seemed to penetrate deep inside of me, causing me to stand frozen in the hallway.

"What kind of doctor are you?" I asked curiously. "You don't fit the traditional mold, if you don't mind me saying."

"A *family* doctor . . . of sorts," came the immediate reply. Much of the young man's figure remained in the shadowed part of the corridor, giving him a look of great mystery.

"From what I can see, you look more like a voodoo doctor...of sorts, "I said with a small laugh. Then, in my most commanding CEO tone, I added: "Well, I have no need for a family doctor, young man. I was in a plane crash. I was hurt very badly. And specialists are about the only people I have any interest in seeing these days. So, I'm sorry, but I'm not interested. I want my old doctor and no one new. And, frankly, your attire makes me feel more than a little uncomfortable. Is that monk's robe you've got on supposed to instill confidence in people?"

"It keeps me warm in the winter," he responded with a smile. "And it reminds me of who I really am," he added.

"And who might that be?" I wondered aloud, taking his bait.

"More about that later. For now just let me say that I have come to help you. You must put all your faith in me. I really do have your best interests in mind."

"Put my faith in you? Are you crazy?" I replied, starting to become angry. "Do you have any idea how much I have suffered? Do you have any idea how much pain I've endured? All I want is my old doctor, some pain pills, and a quiet hospital room. I don't need some joker in a monk's robe telling me he's my new doctor and begging me to trust him."

"I'm not begging you to do anything," the young man stated calmly. "I'm simply informing you that I can help you in ways you cannot imagine. Your old doctor is indeed a very good one. Actually, she's the best in her field and an excellent choice—if it's only your body you want to fix."

"What do you mean by that?" I asked, growing more and more agitated.

"Well, your doctor will help you get your physical health back. But I have come to do so much more for you. I have come here to help you get your life back together." He paused reflectively, seeming to choose his

next few words with great care, then added with exceptional gentleness that made him seem far older than he
appeared to be: "I know that you are facing struggles in
your life—especially with your family. I know that you
have experienced not just a physical crisis but a spiritual
one, too, one that is forcing you to confront the way you
have been living and reconsider the priorities of your
life. I also know that your family means everything to
you and something inside you is telling you to start
putting them first before it is too late."

"How could you possibly know that?" I asked, whispering as I tried to maintain a sense of security in front
of this man who knew so much about me.

"Trust me, I know pretty much everything there is to
know about you. I know where you grew up. I know that
apple pie with a scoop of chocolate ice cream on top is
your favorite dessert and that *Wall Street* is your
favorite movie of all time. I even know about that birth-
mark on your..."

"Stop!" I interjected. "Enough already. I think I get
the point."

Who was this guy? First he flies up and down the
hallway in that wheelchair as if he was on the first lap
of a Formula One racecourse. Then he comes up with
some far-fetched story about being my new "family
doctor." And now he recites details of my personal life
in all-too-accurate detail. I was growing concerned.
Maybe this young man was dangerous.

"Listen. I have no idea who you are and I don't really care all that much," I lied. "I'm tired, I'm in pain, and I need to rest. I suggest you get back into that wheelchair, head back down that hallway and let's forget we ever met. If you don't," I suggested in the most threatening voice I could muster, "I'll have those nurses call security immediately."

The young man remained relaxed and supremely confident. Then he started to laugh. He chuckled at first. Soon he started to roar with laughter.

"Oh, Catherine, if only you could see yourself. Getting mad at a monk in a doctor's robe while you're standing in that silly hospital gown showing no privacy in the back. I've always loved your spunk. You still never let anyone push you around. Glad to see you haven't changed a bit in all these years."

He knew my name. Now I was really worried. I started walking toward the nursing station to get help when the young man raised an arm and grabbed my hand, quickly placing something inside of it.

"Let go of me!" I yelled in an attempt to get the attention of the two nurses working nearby.

"Okay," the young man retreated. "Just give me back my butterfly and I'll be gone."

"Your butterfly? What on earth are you talking about? You really are a lunatic!" I shouted—until I looked down at the object that rested in my hand.

"Where did you get that?" I asked, beginning to calm down. "My dad gave me one of those when I was much younger," I added softly. "He had them specially made for me and my brother, Julian. They were truly unique and original pieces. We'd never seen anything like them before. I thought there were only two of these in the world, to be honest with you. Guess I was wrong."

"There *are* only two of them in the world," came the gentle reply.

I was baffled. If there were only two of these golden butterflies, and I had one at home, and Julian had the other, how could this strange visitor to the hospital have gotten one? I was worried again. Maybe Julian was in trouble.

"Do you my know Julian?" I asked hopefully.

"Better than you could ever imagine. I guess you could say that Julian and I are extraordinarily close," he replied with a grin that suggested he knew far more than he was revealing.

"Where is he?" I asked eagerly.

"He's here," came the reply. "Actually right here in the hospital."

"You're kidding." My heart started to race. I began to feel a little dizzy. My brother, the superstar litigator, his life derailed by tragedy, the man who had headed off to India so many years ago to find himself and save his soul, had returned and was actually here in this very hospital. Impossible.

"Where?" I asked, growing tired of this man's game playing.

"Julian is right in front of your eyes. Julian has returned. Julian is back. And better than before, I might add," replied the young man joyfully, as he did a little jig.

"I'm so sorry," I said sincerely. "I sense that you have good intentions and my intuition tells me you are harmless. But I am at a complete loss as to who you are and why you are here. If you know where Julian is, why won't you tell me where to find him?"

The young man stepped back and raised his hands into a prayer stance as I've observed people in India do upon greeting one another. He stood still and looked deep into my eyes. He did not speak for a moment, and all I could hear was his breathing. A single tear rolled down his cheek. He then appeared to regain his composure and slowly wiped his face with one of the sleeves of his delicate robe before taking a final pause and answering my question.

"Because, dear sister Catherine, I am Julian."

The young man then stepped out of the shadows and, for the first time, walked directly into the light. And though the physical transformation had indeed been extraordinary, there was no doubt in my mind that what I had just heard had been the truth. My dear brother, away on some wild adventure in the Himalayas, had finally returned.

The Miraculous Journey of the Great Julian Mantle

"You who would accomplish little must sacrifice little; you who would achieve much must sacrifice much; you who would attain highly must sacrifice greatly."
—James Allen

I COULD NOT CONTAIN MY EMOTIONS. After so much time apart from the only brother I had, my heart overflowed with joy that he had finally returned. I cried uncontrollably, shedding more tears in those first few minutes than I had in the entire decade prior to this remarkable reunion. As we hugged and kissed, I could scarcely believe how much Julian had changed. How had he achieved this miracle, and what had he experienced while he was away? By my calculations, he would be in his late fifties right now and, frankly, he had looked at least twenty years older than that the last time I had seen him. Back then, his wizened face testified to the extent of his suffering and the burden of his out-of-balance lifestyle. He had been dramatically overweight, coughed incessantly, and often had trouble breathing. It was clear to me then that the old Julian had a death wish and was working himself into the ground as a means to bring it all to an end.

The Julian before me, on the other hand, was a perfect specimen of peak health. His body was strong and his bearing was powerful. His face exuded the energy of youth and an abundance of joy. Even more remarkable were his eyes—unbelievably striking eyes. There was something within them that told me that this young man was an old soul who had seen more and learned more than anyone could ever have imagined of him. He seemed wise and worldly and decent and kind.

"The deepest personal defeat suffered by human beings is constituted by the difference between what one is capable of becoming and what one has in fact become," observed Ashley Montagu. This man standing before me, who embodied great strength yet enormous humility, seemed to be a person who had somehow become all that he was capable of being. I cannot really describe why I had this feeling. Let me just say that at that moment, I had the sense that I was standing before a human being that had connected to his own special form of greatness.

"I know it's impossible to believe, Catherine. But it really is me. God, it's great to see you, little sister. You have no idea how much I've missed you and how often I've thought about you," Julian said as he reached over and gave me yet another bear hug, followed by a tender kiss on my forehead.

"You could have called me or at least written us a letter," I replied.

He paused for a long moment as a pained look came over his face. "I'm so sorry I cut you off like I did, but after Ally died, my heart and spirit broke. I've never felt so much pain in my whole life. Some days I was in so much agony over my loss that I couldn't get out of bed. I didn't want to talk to anyone. I didn't want to see anyone. I did whatever I could to throw myself into my work. It was the only thing that could keep my mind off Ally."

"But we could have helped," I said sincerely.

"I don't think so, Catherine. I was deeply wounded and I really did need to get away from this place. You heard about my heart attack, didn't you?"

"I did," I replied sympathetically as he put his arm around me and we started walking back into my room.

"Well, it almost killed me. The doctors said it was a miracle that I survived. They said that I had a brave heart and a burning will to live. After the heart attack, there was no way in the world I was going back to my law practice. The passion and sense of focus had evaporated and I had a hunger for something else."

"Like what?"

"I had a thirst to discover a much deeper sense of meaning in my life. In this age we live in, we hear it spoken about a lot. So many of us are asking ourselves life's bigger questions, like what is it all about and why am I here and what is the true purpose of my existence on this planet?"

"I've noticed that too, Julian."

"Hey, that's the first time you've called me Julian, little sister. You really do believe it's me!"

"I do. But your transformation is pretty amazing." I then reached over, kissed Julian on his bronzed cheek, and gave him another huge hug. He reciprocated with a kiss to my forehead and we held each other close, feeling that unique human connection that only brothers and sisters can share. As we hugged each other, I noticed Julian starting to shake. As I looked up at his face, I saw that he had started to cry once again. This made me cry, too, and soon tears were flowing down both our faces.

Julian quickly reined in his emotion, but I noticed none of the embarrassment that the Julian of old would have shown at this outburst of vulnerability. "You've never seen me cry as an adult, have you, Catherine?"

"True."

"One of the many things I've learned while I've been away is that we all need to be real."

"To be real?" I asked, not quite sure of what Julian was getting at.

"Yes, Catherine. Most of us live our entire lives wearing a social mask that hides our true selves. Rather than showing the full colors of our humanity, we work hard to sculpt an image of the person we think the world wants us to be. We say the things other people want us to say and wear the clothes other people want us to wear and do the things other people want us to do. Rather than living the lives we have been destined to live, we end up living the lives of other people. And in so doing, we die a slow death. *'Death is only one of many ways of dying,'* the explorer Alvah Simon put it. So now, I live my life entirely according to what my heart tells me is the right way to live. If I feel like crying, as I just did because I am so happy to be with you again, I cry. If I feel over- whelmed with joy, I sing. If I feel love toward someone, I express it. I guess you could say that I now wear my heart on my sleeve. I live completely in the moment and enjoy every single moment of this great gift we call life."

"And that means you are 'real'?" I asked.

"Yes, it means that I am living the way we were made to live. Too many people become domesticated."

"Domesticated?"

"Sure. They have become so good at keeping up appearances and doing what others expect of them that they become domesticated—like trained seals."

"Isn't that a little harsh, Julian?"

"Not really, Catherine. *We all have a high human duty to live our lives out loud. We all have a deep human obligation to live our best lives and show up at the top of our game every single day.* That means being real and listening to your inner wisdom. It means saying no to all those things that you know are not the right things for you to do, so you can say yes to all those true priorities that will add great richness to your days and true fulfillment to your hours." Julian continued. "I could have gone back to practicing law, but it would have been a personal defeat."

"How so?"

"Because I have learned through my trials in life that everything that happens to us happens to us for a reason."

"I agree completely," I said, recognizing this to be a principle I had recently discovered in my own life.

"Not only that, but I have also learned that failures and suffering in life are actually our best friends. Alexander Graham Bell made the point well when he remarked: 'When one door closes, another opens. But we often look so long and so regretfully upon the closed door that we fail to see the one that has opened for us,'" offered Julian, concentrating on his words as he spoke.

"So true," I stated.

"Yes, Catherine. *Our wounds ultimately give us wisdom. Our stumbling blocks inevitably become our stepping stones. And our setbacks lead us to our strengths.* As Leighton once wrote: 'Adversity is the diamond dust that heaven polishes its jewels with.'"

"Lovely words. Let me write them down," I said earnestly.

"You won't need to, little sister. I'll teach you everything you need to know and believe me, you won't forget a thing. But here's the point I'm trying to make: I could have gone back to practicing law and making all that money. But to have done so would have been to turn a blind eye to the opportunity that life had presented me with. There must have been some reason for Ally's death and my divorce and my subsequent heart attack. I knew that if I accepted the challenge and got out of the pity party I had been spending my days in, I would discover something that would take me to a whole new level of living. And I sensed that with this would come far more joy, happiness, and love than I had ever known."

"Love? I don't remember you being much of one to speak about love, Julian. My, how you have changed."

"Love is what we need more of in this world, Catherine. And I'm not only referring to loving other people. We must show love to our work. We must show love to our surroundings, and most importantly, we must show love to ourselves. Only then can we really give our love fully to other people. My point of wisdom is simply this: *everything you do as you live out your days must speak of love*. Leo Tolstoy wrote: 'Only one clear quality marks an action as either good or evil: if it increases the amount of love in the world, it is good. If it separates people and creates animosity among them, it is bad.'"

"So to be more fully human I should not only show more love to Jon, the kids and all the people around me, but I should also show love to my work? Then I'll be a real, fully functioning person. But doesn't that lead to the very imbalance I have been struggling with for so long? I don't think I should be working more. I think I should be working less."

"Interesting observation, Catherine. Well, I guess it all comes down to what you describe to be your work. You are speaking of work in a very narrow way. I am speaking of loving the work of your life."

"My life's work?"

"Yes. Perhaps for you your life's work is raising two fine children who will go out into this world and make it a better, wiser place. I also sense your life's work involves BraveLife.com and the lives you are transforming with that enterprise."

"How do you know about BraveLife.com?" I asked in amazement. "I thought you had sequestered yourself in some mountain retreat high in the Himalayas."

"Since I've been back, I've been reading about you. You've been doing some great things on the business front, little sister, not that I'm at all surprised. I must have taught you well," Julian suggested with mock pride.

"Don't stick that muscled chest you've somehow acquired out too far, big brother. I did it all myself," I laughed.

"Always the independent one, Catherine. I've always loved that in you as well as your toughness and that dedication to excellence that you have always insisted upon. But back to what I was saying—love your life's work. Love everything and everyone. Your life will change."

"Do you have an example?"

"Well, how about if I offer you the words of that great philosopher Kahlil Gibran. His words are so beautiful to me: 'When you work, you are a flute whose heart the whispering of the hours turns to music. To love life through labor is to be intimate with life's utmost secret. All work is empty save when there is love, for work is love made visible.' So love your work at BraveLife. Give yourself to it and add value to lives in the process. But also love your work as a mother and your role as a partner to Jon."

"Okay," I replied in complete fascination. "So what exactly did you do after the heart attack?"

"Well, first I made a conscious decision to sell everything I owned. I had to travel light, and all my worldly possessions would only clutter my mind and encumber my life. I decided to strip my life down to the very essentials of human existence and to simplify to the core. And so I sold the mansion. I sold the plane. I sold the island."

"You even sold your Ferrari, Julian. I couldn't believe it when I heard you did that!"

"I think I even surprised myself with that little gesture," Julian noted with a smile as he stroked the embroidery on the sleeve of his beautiful robe.

"I headed off to India, a place I knew would hold many of the answers to the questions that I needed to ask. That was an incredibly spiritual period of my life. I felt liberated for the first time in years. I knew that I was embarking on some great path that would lead me to a whole new understanding of what life was all about. George Bernard Shaw wrote that 'to be in hell is to drift; to be in heaven is to steer,' and for the first time in so very long, I actually felt I was in control of my future. I felt as if I was living by design rather than by default— the way so many of us live our lives."

"I agree, Julian. Most people seem to live their lives by accident, reacting to the events of their days rather than creating the circumstances they see in their dreams," I added, becoming caught up in the inspiration my brother was filling me with.

"Beautifully said, Catherine. Oh, I am impressed!" he shouted with enthusiasm, slapping both of his bronzed hands on his knees. "You've always had a superb mind, but now you've developed a poet's heart."

"Well, not quite, Julian," I replied humbly.

Julian then recounted how he had traveled across India, sometimes by train, sometimes by bicycle, and sometimes on foot. He delighted in meeting the people of that rich culture and learning their wise ways. He visited ancient temples and watched majestic sunsets over ancient ruins. He began to reconnect with the childlike spirit he had lost sight of, and gradually his trademark smile returned.

"I used to stare at the stars for hours. I devoured philosophical texts, making notes in my dog-eared journal about all the insights that came to me. I used to take long walks with sages and yogis and pepper them with question after question about what life's highest purpose really was and how I could fill my days with more meaning and grace. I asked them how one could be healthier and happier and more alive to life before it was too late. I wondered how I could deepen my human relationships and find the love I had lost after Ally died and my wife left me. And I encouraged them to teach me how to slow down my noisy mind and discover a deep sense of inner peace that I knew was one of the cornerstones of a truly fulfilling life."

"Sounds like a remarkable time, Julian. I especially like the stuff about slowing down and enjoying the more fundamental pleasures of life that we all miss out on as we keep up the crazy pace of this new world we exist in. I recently clipped out a quote from the newspaper. Here, let me show it to you," I said, reaching down into the drawer of the table at my bedside. It read:

Most of us miss out on life's big prizes. The Pulitzer. The Nobel. Oscars. Tonys. Emmys. But we are all eligible for life's small pleasures. A pat on the back. A kiss behind the ear. A four-pound bass. A full moon. An empty parking space. A crackling fire. A great meal. A glorious sunset. Hot soup. Cold beer. Don't fret about getting life's grand awards. Enjoy its tiny delights. There are plenty for all of us.

"Oooh, that's really good, Catherine. I wish I'd written that. Really makes the point of enjoying the basic blessings of life as our path unfolds. I've now learned that the road really is as good as the end, and it is so important that we not put off being happy until the arrival of some future event. Too many of us lie to ourselves in this respect."

"Please clarify?"

"Sure, we tell ourselves that we will be happy when we get that big promotion or that new job. Or we say we will have more fun in life once the kids grow up and go off to college. We say we will make the time to watch the stars and pursue our passions when we retire. But that is the Big Lie of Life. *Happiness does not arrive when you achieve certain things. It comes when you think certain thoughts. Happiness is nothing more than a state of mind that you create by the way that you process and interpret the events of your life.* It comes by giving great thanks for all that you have in your life and from developing the Gratitude Mind-set whereby you deeply appreciate all the little wonders of your life. As the sage thinker Cecil once observed: 'Every year of my life, I grow more convinced that it is wisest and best to fix our attention on the beautiful and the good and dwell as little as possible on the evil and false.'"

"Even more important, remember that the hand that gives is the hand that gathers, and that giving to others starts the receiving process. Do not make happiness the goal that drives you. Make service to others and a heartfelt desire to enrich people your core focus—then happiness will come. 'Just imagine that the purpose of life is your happiness only—then life becomes a cruel and senseless thing,' wrote Tolstoy. 'You have to embrace what the wisdom of humanity, your intellect, and your heart tell you: that the meaning of life is to serve the force that sent you into the world. Then life becomes a joy.'"

"Powerful words. I'll need to think more about them when I am alone. But now, please tell me more about your journey. It's an incredible story."

"After a few months of some of the most intense personal growth and discovery I have ever experienced," Julian continued. "I began to grow hungry for even more meaningful wisdom on how to live a richer, more joy-filled life. I pushed the teachers and pundits I had met to reveal even deeper truths to me and to help me find even greater enlightenment. They were so decent and loving, sharing everything they knew without even the slightest expectation of anything in return. I now know they were aligned with what is known as the Abundance Principle."

"The Abundance Principle. I've never heard of it," I replied with great curiosity as I sat up straight in my bed.

"It's that timeless and immutable principle of nature that I've just hinted at. It holds that *the more you give to others, the more you will ultimately receive yourself.* I've discovered that if you want more abundance and prosperity in life, you need to give more. Abundance is an energy that circulates in the world, and the more you send out, the more you will see come back to you. The Abundance Principle works incredibly well in business as well. To grow wealthy, stop wishing that you made more money and ask yourself how you can help more people. When you get deeply focused and committed to adding value to the lives of those people you serve, the money will begin to flow in a river. Never forget, Catherine, that money is nothing more than payment from the universe for value added and services rendered. The more value you can add, the more money you will make."

"So you are saying that people in business make a mistake in making the pursuit of money their primary objective?"

"I am. Money is not to be chased. Money is the *by-product* that can flow into your life when your focus shifts to helping people live better lives and realize their own dreams. As Viktor Frankl wrote so perfectly: 'Success, like happiness, cannot be pursued. It must ensue. And it only does so as the unintended side of one's personal dedication to a cause greater than one's self.'"

Julian added: "In India, amid such wisdom and love for humanity, I realized that there is a grand purpose to every life."

"Really?"

"Truly, little sister. We are all here to live heroic lives and make a difference to the world, in our own unique way. I recently came across the words of General James Doolittle of the U.S. Air Force, who made the point of wisdom I'm trying to convey in these terms: '*We were put on earth for one purpose and that is to make it a better place. We should, therefore, be contributing members of society. And if the earth, as a result of our having been on it, is a better place than it was before we came, then we have achieved our destiny.*'"

"Then why don't more of us discover this calling? Why are so many of us unfulfilled and unhappy?"

"Because we are so busy filling our lives with clutter and possessions and busyness that we have no time to think about The Things That Truly Count. It reminds me of the words of an ancient Zen master who reflected: 'Most people try to get more every day while I strive to grow simpler and more uncomplicated every day.' If we would only slow down, press the pause button a little more often, and have a look at the big picture of our lives, we would arrive at a greater understanding of why we are here and what we must be doing. I know the last thing you want to hear about is being on a plane, but there's a metaphor I need to share with you."

"You're right. I'm still quite fearful about flying, but go ahead."

"Don't worry, Catherine. I've spoken to all your doctors and even had some of my old friends, the best doctors in the country, review your charts and check your progress. Everyone advises me you are doing extremely well and will make a full recovery. I know you've gone through a great tragedy and, believe me, the very purpose of my visit is to help you through this whole thing. But the point I want to make is simply this: on a plane, let's say at 35,000 feet, if you look down to the ground, you gain a complete perspective on the world. You cannot miss the forest for the trees because you get the full view."

"I agree. We see the big picture."

"Right. Well, what we need to do far more often in our lives is to 'go up to 35,000.'"

"We need to fly more?" I asked, slightly confused.

"No, what I'm saying is that we need to regain perspective in our lives so we can identify and then realign the way we live with our most important priorities. We need to 'go up to 35,000' so we can have a eagle's-eye view of the way we are conducting our days so we can make those essential course corrections and get back on track toward our destination. Most people just don't do enough of that. As the thinker Joanna Smith Bers said:

We need to define our priorities—the values, endeavors, and dreams that guide us—and build our worlds around those things. It's not enough just to get through the day. We need to make every day a platform for accomplishing what we want out of life. We must take responsibility for ourselves and the world we live in so that we can live with ourselves and the world around us.

"Hmm," I replied. Never before had anyone been able to share wisdom that struck me so clearly. Thoughts began racing through my head as I identified all the things that were not working in my life and all the priorities that I had been neglecting for so long. Mostly I thought about my family. I really missed Porter and Sarita. I wondered if Jon was okay and what he would be doing at home right now. I started making more promises to myself about the changes I would make and all the new actions I would take the moment I was released from this hospital room. Then my mind drifted back to Julian. My brother had become so much more than the person he once had been. The former Julian was brilliant and tenacious and charismatic. But the new Julian was thoughtful and knowing and wise. I loved him even more this way.

"So you were saying that you kept on pressing the pundits you met for even deeper knowledge, Julian. What happened?"

"I learned some amazing things and discovered things about myself I'd never known before."

By this time, Julian was relaxing on the chair next to my bed with his long legs outstretched and his hands resting comfortably behind his head. His face was animated as he spoke, and his eyes danced with the passion of his message. I was spellbound by what my brother was saying and mesmerized by every word he spoke.

"After a few months of traveling into the north of India, I started hearing whisperings about a band of monks who lived high in the Himalayas. According to legend, these sages, known only as 'The Great Sages of Sivana'—Sivana means 'oasis of enlightenment' in their language—had developed an extraordinary system that anyone could use to achieve remarkable levels of personal mastery and inner fulfillment. These sages had distilled all of the wisdom of the ages into a practical and extremely powerful process that they used to live their lives with a remarkable degree of peace, joy, and festivity. The only problem was that nobody seemed to know how to find these elusive monks. I also heard that many had died trying.

"Anyway," continued Julian as he took a sip of tea from my cup, "you know I've always believed in taking risks. It's like Dad always told us: 'At the end of our lives, what we will regret the most will not be all the risks we took. What will fill our hearts with the greatest amount of sadness will be all those risks we didn't take, all those fears we didn't face, and all those wonderful opportunities we did not seize.' Remember, Catherine, *on the other side of fear lies freedom.* So I threw caution to the wind and with every ounce of enthusiasm I could muster up I headed off for the Himalayas in search of the ultimate knowledge I was committed to discovering. And if I didn't find the monks, I was prepared to die trying.

"For many days and many nights, I climbed in those treacherous mountains. Though I endured great pain and came close to death on more than one occasion, I also experienced beauty I'd never seen before," remarked Julian. "I guess it was the rawness of the scenery and the simplicity of my surroundings that touched me so deeply. I felt so connected to the universe on that trek and a part of something so much larger than myself up there. And I never gave up. I just climbed and climbed, hoping I would survive and eventually find the sages. You know I've always believed that persistence is a quality that needs to be cultivated within every one of us if we hope to get to where we dream of going in life. 'Some succeed because they are destined to; most succeed because they are determined to,' noted Anatole France.

"After much effort and dedication, I finally had a breakthrough. One day, I caught a glimpse of another figure, dressed oddly in a long flowing red robe topped by a dark blue hood. I could not believe another person could be up here alone. 'For what purpose could someone be up here?' I wondered.

"I yelled out to this fellow climber but rather than stopping to talk to me, the figure started moving even more quickly up the mountain path we were ascending. When I called out again, this time at the top of my lungs, the strange traveler started to run at full speed, his face still hidden from view, his red robe dancing gracefully in the wind behind him.

"'Please, friend, I'm in great distress!' I cried out. 'I need your help to find Sivana. I'm looking for the sages, and I think I'm lost!'

"Then the figure came to an abrupt stop. As I moved closer to this mysterious person whose face was still hidden by the hood, the traveler turned toward me and began stepping in my direction. Suddenly, a burst of sunlight struck the face, revealing that the traveler was a man. But I must tell you, Catherine, I've never seen a man quite like this one. Never. My guess was that he was probably in his late fifties, but his brown face was supple and smooth. His body looked remarkably strong and powerful, and he radiated boundless vitality. He stood tall and had an almost regal bearing about him. And I still remember his eyes, so penetrating that I was compelled to look away for an instant.

"It was obvious to me that my search had come to an end. I was convinced; this had to be one of the Great Sages of Sivana. And so I opened my heart to this human being, praying for his help and explaining why I had risked my life to come up to this perilous place. I told him about my former life, the success I had experienced as a superstar in the legal world, the jetset lifestyle I had adopted, and then of the tremendous loss I had endured on the death of Ally. I pleaded with him to take me to his community of sages and to permit me to learn from their deep wisdom so I could discover the secrets of a complete, meaningful life."

Julian told me that the man listened to his tale with intense concentration without speaking a word. He was not even sure if the sage understood a word he was saying. Then, surprisingly, the sage reached over and put an arm on my brother's shoulder. "If you truly have a heartfelt desire to learn the wisdom of a better way to live out your life, then it is my personal duty to help you. I will never refuse to assist anyone who comes to me in need. Giving help to one who requires assistance is one of our sacred vows and one that I hold close to my heart. I am indeed one of those sages you have come so far in search of. You are the first person to find us in many years. Congratulations, I admire your tenacity. You must have been quite a lawyer," he remarked with a grin. The sage then led Julian to the mountain hideaway where he and the other monks lived, promising him that they would welcome him with open arms and teach him the ancient principles that their ancestors had passed down to them over the ages.

"There was one condition that this sage imposed on me, however," noted Julian seriously. "I still remember his words: 'Before I take you into our private world and share our collective knowledge, I must ask for one promise from you. Although we are isolated here in these magical mountains, we are acutely aware of the turmoil your world is in. People are forgetting how to live with decency and love. People have lost sight of the things that truly count. They sacrifice meaning for money and chase profit instead of purpose. Their families are no longer their highest priority and, as a consequence, their spouses and their children suffer needlessly. They no longer make the time to renew themselves and cultivate their most important human relationships. They have forgotten that life's little pleasures, like the magic of a child's laugh or the glory of a sunrise, are life's most important ones. I feel so strongly that people in your part of the world deserve to lead happier and fuller lives. I know there is hope for all these people, and my intuition is telling me that this hope must come from you. While you are with us in these mystical mountains, you will discover a remarkable system for true leadership of your life. You will learn so much about the power that the human spirit has to be a force for good in this chaotic world. You will discover how to be stronger, healthier, happier, and wiser than you have ever been. You will also come to understand how important rich relationships are for effective living, and learn some very unique techniques to restore a true sense of love for your life."

"Love?" Julian asked, surprised that the sage would value this.

"Yes," came the quick reply. "We all need more love in our lives. As a matter of fact, this world would be a far better place with more love. But before I take you into our culture and introduce you to all my brothers and sisters, you must first promise me that you will share the lessons you learn at our feet with all those in the West who need to hear them. You must be the conduit of the ancient life wisdom we have accumulated and spread it throughout your world so that many people can be helped and many lives will be transformed. Most important in life is not what you get from it, but what you give to it. Life is about helping others and blessing the world by the way you live. You must commit yourself from the deepest core of your heart to governing the rest of your days with this simple but forgotten principle. Promise?"

"I agreed to this condition immediately," Julian told me, before taking a pause. "Within a few hours I was standing in the most amazing village I had ever seen in my life. It was breathtakingly beautiful and surreal in its appearance. Never seen anything even close to that place, Catherine. Every structure, including the temple that rested in the center of the village, was covered by roses."

"Roses?" I questioned.

"Roses. I mean the fragrance of that place was so incredible. And every one of the inhabitants of Sivana looked just as special as the great sage who had brought me there. I was in complete awe of the whole place. I really couldn't believe it. I had risked my life to find this legendary place. I had finally found it, and then I was given the privilege of being a part of their community and the chance to study at their feet. The joy I felt moved me to tears."

Julian's story had held me enthralled for nearly two hours. My brother's adventure was the stuff of fiction, and yet he had actually lived it. For some reason, the nurses outside my room had decided to leave us alone, perhaps sensing that he was family and that the contact would be good for my spirits. I wondered what they thought of his attire? Probably the first monk they have seen in here, I giggled. I couldn't wait to hear what Julian had learned in Sivana. I now know why he had said he had returned here to help me. He had come back home to fulfill his promise to the sage by sharing their system of life renewal and wise living with me. I hoped Julian could help me mend my family relationships and teach me how to make my home the spirited place I knew it could be. For the first time in a long while, I felt excited at the prospect of a more fulfilling life. The emptiness that had engulfed me for so long started to pass like gray storm clouds making way for the first rays of sunshine. Julian stood up.

"Catherine, I'm so happy to see you," he said tenderly. "But I have to leave for a little while. There are some things that I have to do."

"Julian, I haven't seen you in years. Please don't leave me now," I replied anxiously.

"I promise I'll be back. As a matter of fact, I have no plans to leave here anytime soon, so you're stuck with me whether you like it or not. You've probably guessed why I'm here."

"To fulfill your promise to the sages?"

"Exactly. I knew you were in trouble. I read about the plane crash, and that was why I rushed here. But even before that, I knew you were spiraling downwards into darkness. I heard from one of my former law partners that you had become a great success in business but that your personal life was in shambles. Those two fine children of yours need you. You have an obligation to put them first and to inspire them to develop the leadership qualities that will help them become great, caring adults one day. I will show you how to become a masterful parent and find deep fulfillment in the process. I will share the sages' secrets of building relationships so your connection to Jon deepens in profound ways. And I'll also teach you how to simplify that complex life of yours and restore ideal balance."

"Do you think I have to give up my career?" I asked.

"Not at all. I'm here to teach you that it is possible to have it all. It is possible to have a satisfying professional life where you do great work and touch many lives and, at the same time, raise a wonderful family while creating a rich home culture. As a matter of fact," added Julian, "I've discovered that building a strong foundation at home will fuel even greater success at work."

"Is it really possible to be superb in both areas of life?"

"Absolutely," responded Julian as he started to walk toward the door. "The trick is to work smarter, not harder. You need to bring a greater sense of *focus* to your work and gain greater clarity about which activities are essential and which ones are not. That will free up time for your family as well as time for all the self-care activities that will restore inner peace and joy in your days. But more about that later. I've got places to go and people to meet," said Julian with a big grin. "I wonder what those models I used to date would think of the robe?" he mused.

"You're kidding, right?"

"Of course I am, Catherine. I have become a man who walks his talk and lives his message. *We all need to live our message.* My own life is much different from the one you once knew me to lead. I live simply and to the point, concentrating only on life's essentials. My wild days are over."

"Glad to hear that, brother. Boy, I used to worry about you."

"Not anymore. Thanks, little sister. Love ya!"

And with that, the legal superstar turned enlightened monk kissed me on the forehead once again and darted out of the room, his red robe swaying behind him. All that remained of this most surprising visit was a single object that he had left next to my pillow. It was his golden butterfly. As I turned it over, I could see that Julian had, in tiny writing, engraved some words upon it. I put on my reading glasses and read the elegantly inscripted message. *"Catherine,"* it said, *"your children are the greatest blessings of your life and they will only be young once. Put them first and your life will soar. I'm so happy to be home. Your fan, Julian."*

The First Mastery
of the Family Leader™

Leadership in Life Begins with Leadership at Home

"Twenty-five years ago I wish someone had told me that the enduring meaning in my life would be found in shaping my children's values, not in my professional success."
—Rabbi Harold Kushner

"If children grew up according to early indications, we should have nothing but geniuses."
—Goethe

IT HAD BEEN JUST UNDER A MONTH since I had returned home from the hospital. Thankfully, just as Julian had promised, I had made a full recovery and regained all the strength and stamina that had been so much a part of who I was in the past. But so many other things changed as a result of my wake-up call at 35,000 feet. I'd decided to streamline my work life and set up a home office in our basement. Instantly my previous full-hour commute was transformed into one lasting a full minute. And I loved being able to conduct transatlantic conference calls with CEOs from major firms while I was standing in my flannel pajamas. Though my priorities had been reconfigured, I still loved the adrenaline rush that running a business gave me, and I felt grateful that Julian had advised me not to give up this aspect of my life.

On doctor's orders, I started a serious exercise regimen—which made me feel great—and I adopted a much healthier diet. No more late night pit stops at the drive-through windows or three-cheese pizzas with double pepperoni and bacon. I began spending most of my time at home with Jon and the kids and really dedicated myself to rekindling the spark that had been lost during all my time away. And one of the biggest changes of all: Julian, the former owner of one of the the city's biggest mansions, and a man known for his fierce independence, moved in with us, setting up home in the small but sun-soaked room above the garage. I guess he really was committed to *living his message,* and since he preached the power of a simple life, I was pleased to see that he now practiced it. I'll admit, though, that it was hard for me to believe that my brother, the legendary Julian Mantle, having returned from his extraordinary trek through the Himalayas where he met the world's most remarkable sages, was now living quietly in the granny quarters above our garage. Life can yield such bizarre outcomes.

And yet I must also tell you that I did not feel any sorrow or pity for my brother. Of course I felt sad that life had dealt him such hard blows. The loss of his daughter, Ally, was far more than he deserved. It's just that in my mind, I didn't feel that he had fallen from grace. Sure, he no longer sported about town in his gleaming Ferrari, had sold his opulent mansion, and was now living in a crawlspace only slightly bigger than the bathroom of his former office. Sure, he was no longer the toast of the town, spending late nights with beautiful fashion models barely into their twenties and hipper-than-hip investment bankers who thought nothing of jetting down to Nassau for a night at the casino. I guess I felt that while he no longer had the material trappings of his former life, he seemed to have found something far more important. Julian's health was superb, the lively spirit of his boyhood had returned, and he had become the keeper of wisdom so substantial it made me quiver. To me, his life had gone from total complexity to utter simplicity. It had shifted from an existence of constant frustration to one of jubilant celebration. No, Julian had not fallen from grace. He had discovered it.

"Let's go down to the BraveLife.com headquarters," said Julian as he strolled into our sunny kitchen one day after completing the ritual walk he took every morning as the day broke. "I haven't been in an office tower for years, and I'm curious to see how things have changed in the corporate world."

Although I now worked out of our home, all our employees remained in the luxurious offices that my partners and I had leased when we started the company—before they died. We had two floors in one of the city's most prestigious skyscrapers with a view that would take your breath away. While I would visit the office periodically, I soon came to dread going downtown.

"Why in the world would you want to go there, Julian? You haven't even spoken to your old friends in years. I would have thought that the financial district—the place you practically lived when you were Mr. Big Shot Lawyer—would be the last place you'd want to go."

"Actually, I have spoken to a couple of my friends since I've returned from the Himalayas, but that's another story," replied Julian mysteriously. "And I really do need to go downtown."

"What do you need? You know I'm happy to pick up anything you want."

"Actually, it's not for me that I want to go downtown—it's for you."

"For me? I have no interest in heading down there. I'm

happy working from home and everyone's doing just fine at the office without me. And anyway," I continued, "you'll never get past security in that robe you insist on wearing every day. Are you sure you want to keep wearing it? Everyone on the street is talking about 'the monk who moved in with the Cruz family.' Even Miss Williamson, the old woman who sits in her dark living room all day with her fourteen cats, walked up to me as I was doing some gardening out front and asked me who you were. I'll bet she thinks you're cute, Julian," I mocked.

"She's not my type," Julian retorted with a laugh. "Trust me on this one, Catherine," he continued. "There's a lesson I want to share with you today, and your old office is the perfect place to do it. Actually, there are Five Masteries I plan on sharing with you—*The Five Masteries of the Family Leader,* to be precise."

"What's a mastery?"

"A mastery is a skill that a person becomes brilliant at through continuous focus and constant practice. Over the coming weeks, I will share with you five timeless— and fundamental—philosophies that will completely transform your abilities as a parent and the quality of your family life. *The Five Masteries of the Family Leader* are based directly on the teachings of the Great Sages of Sivana. I've just added some of my own learnings for good measure," Julian said with a knowing smile. "Today I feel you are ready to discover the First Mastery."

"Which is?" I asked with bated breath.

"That *Leadership in Life Begins with Leadership at Home*."

"Fascinating. Tell me more."

"Not until we get downtown," Julian responded firmly. "The setting needs to be perfect."

"Okay, let's go. I know that the *The Five Masteries* are going to change my life. I can just feel it. I truly sense that this wisdom you are sharing with me will revolutionize my thoughts, my words, and my actions," I replied, grabbing my car keys. "And I guess it's about time I start taking some risks again."

"That's the spirit, little sister. Life's all about gaining new knowledge and taking bigger risks, isn't it? The greatest risk in life lies in not taking greater and greater risks."

"Wasn't it Peter Drucker who said that 'there is the risk you cannot afford to take and there is the risk you cannot afford not to take'?"

"Right. And to go back even farther in time, the Roman philosopher Seneca stated that 'it is not because things are difficult that we do not dare. It is because we do not dare that things are difficult.' In my own life I try and take a reasonable risk, even a small one, each and every day. That way, I grow and progress daily."

"I saw the movie *Rounders* on video a few weeks ago. Did you see it?"

"Haven't seen a movie in years, little sister. We monks generally don't spend much time around the VCR," Julian said with a grin so big I thought his face might split. "Anyway, the popcorn always used to get stuck to my teeth. Right in here," he added, opening his mouth and pointing to a crevice between two of the teeth located at the back of his mouth.

"Spare me the gory details, Julian. Anyway, it was a pretty good movie—all about the importance of taking calculated risks in life and pursuing your destiny, even when it's not the easiest thing to do."

"Sounds fascinating."

"It was. Anyway, in the movie, Pappa Wallenda . . ."

"The great high-wire walker?" Julian interjected enthusiastically.

"Yes, the great tightrope walker, Julian. Anyway, Pappa Wallenda was quoted in this movie as saying: 'Life is lived out on the wire. The rest is just waiting.'"

"Oh, that's good. Really good. And it's completely true, Catherine. The people who get on in life are those who dream big dreams and then take whatever risks are necessary to bring their vision to life. They face their fears directly, get into the game and live their days with courage. They break through their fear doors, no matter how scared they feel. Remember, *it's better to be a lion for a day than a sheep all your life.*"

"Wow, that's a powerful expression, Julian."

"And so," Julian continued without a pause, "although I know it will not be easy for you to head down to BraveLife.com after being away for so long, please take the chance. The rewards are sure to flow."

"Feel the fear and do it anyway?"

"Exactly. As I told you in the hospital, *on the other side of fear you will always discover freedom.*"

I felt nervous as Julian and I walked into the gleaming office tower I once spent my best waking hours in. The very smell of the place set my heart aflutter. A security guard approached Julian and I as we made our way to the bank of elevators that would take us to the BraveLife.com corporate offices perched atop this steel and glass monument.

"Hi, Mrs. Cruz. Nice to see you again. I heard about the plane crash. All of us here at the security station were really sad to hear about it. I'm sorry about your partners. They were nice fellas."

"Yes, Matt, they were good men and I miss them a lot. Thanks for mentioning them. I guess it helps me to deal with their loss when I hear how kind they were to so many people. It's good to see you, too. I don't get down here much these days. I'm running the company from my home now so I can spend more time with my family. It sure feels strange to come back."

"That's quite a change, Mrs. Cruz. I'd say that out of everyone I know in this tower, you worked the hardest. Me and the other guards used to place bets on how early you'd get in here and how late you'd leave."

"Well, those days are history, Matt," I replied self-consciously.

"Your children must be happy about your decision. I've got three young ones at home, and I know that the best thing I can do for them as a parent is to spend lots of time with them."

"You're right, Matt. My children are thrilled to have their mom back. To be honest, I've never seen them happier."

The guard's face then tightened. "Sorry to ask this, Mrs. Cruz, but does the gentleman with you have some ID? As you know, this is a high-security building, and I've got to ask that question or my boss will kill me." He then glanced at Julian. "No offense, buddy, but we don't get a lot of monks in here."

"Matt, this is my brother Julian. Julian Mantle."

"Julian Mantle? The famous trial lawyer?"

"Yup, the famous trial lawyer."

The security guard was speechless. "Uh . . . hello, Mr. Mantle. I used to read about you all the time in the papers. I was a really big fan of yours," he added, shaking Julian's hand with both of his own, the way people do when they wish to curry favor. "Some of those cases you won were unbelievable, man. Remember that case where you sued that fast-food restaurant for millions of dollars when hot coffee spilled into your client's lap?"

"I do remember that one, Matt. That was a fun case to win," replied Julian graciously.

"What happened to all those fancy suits you used to wear, Mr. Mantle? And that slick red Ferrari? Man, that was one sweet car. Me and the boys used to see you fly by here with the top down all the time. Those women you had next to you made us drool," the security guard noted with all the exuberance of a schoolboy set to go out on his first date.

"Ancient history, my friend, ancient history," replied Julian, looking away as if he was embarrassed by how ostentatious his previous lifestyle had been.

"Are you a monk now?" persisted the security guard.

"These robes are the clothes I've chosen to wear, Matt. My teachers wore these clothes. They remind me of the man that I now am and the mission that I am dedicated to pursuing. I've chosen to live a far simpler life now. No more Ferraris," said Julian as he patted the security guard on the back and walked toward the elevators.

"Well, go on up, Mr. Mantle. It's an honor to meet you, sir. And you take care, Mrs. Cruz. Have fun with those kids. They'll be all grown up before you know it."

As Julian and I entered the opulent offices that were home to BraveLife.com, I was struck by the sheer busy-ness of the scene in front of me. It seemed that people were just busy being busy. Employees were rushing from place to place, computers were humming, the phones were ringing and faxes were flying.

"Hard to believe this used to be my life," I mentioned to Julian softly.

"Don't be too hard on yourself, Catherine. You had a mortgage to cover and bills to pay. Believe me, I have great empathy for people of this age we live in. Expenses are high and their financial obligations seem endless. They want to provide all the good things in life for their families, so they feel compelled to work longer and harder. And this eventually sucks the life out of them. They become shells of their former selves. By the end of the day, they drive home in their grief containers, crawl into their homes, grunt at their families, and drift off to sleep in their La-Z-Boys. I feel so sad for such people."

"What's a grief container?"

"Oh," Julian replied, starting to giggle, "that's my term for a car. Most people are so unhappy by the time they've finished a miserable day at work, their cars become nothing more than 'grief containers' that transport them home."

I laughed. Julian continued, enjoying how I was concentrating intently on his every word.

"Such people are living half-lives, Catherine. 'One of the saddest experiences that can come to a human being is to awaken, gray-haired and wrinkled, near the close of an unproductive life, to the fact that all through the years he has been using only a small part of himself,' V.W. Burrows noted. And that's the point of wisdom here. The name of the game is not to sacrifice yourself for work and have nothing left for the people you truly love. Change the rules—no, break all the rules and realize that the whole idea is to work for the sake of living rather than living for the sake of work. Be superb at work. Have a great time at it and dedicate yourself to helping your clients. But have the wisdom to realize that there is more to life than the nice things money can buy. How about having nice kids and a nice family and a loving home life? Those things can only come when you devote yourself to enriching your home culture. And that, my little sister, takes time. *Never forget that the best gift you can ever give your kids is the gift of your time.*"

"Really?"

"Absolutely. It shows them that you truly love and value them. Nothing else is as precious or as important. Which brings me to why I've brought you down here."

"I was wondering about that."

"What is BraveLife.com?"

"It's a company that trains the employees of our client organizations to be more productive, effective, and far more successful in the way they work. We are the Internet's premier e-learning firm."

"Anything else?"

"Our unique technology allows employees to receive coaching from the best experts on the planet conveniently at their very own desktops."

"Is that your final answer?" Julian asked, grinning like a game show host.

"Yes."

"All of those answers are correct. But the one I was really looking for was this one: at the end of the day, your company is a community."

"Really?"

"Sure, it is. Ultimately, the company that you have so tirelessly dedicated yourself to building is nothing more than an assembly of human beings united to pursue a common cause. BraveLife.com is not really a corporate entity. It is a collection of people working toward the same aim."

"Making money?" I asked, surprised by my own cynicism.

"No, not at all. They all crave meaning. They all crave a feeling of fulfillment. And they all ache, whether they realize it or not, for what I call a Compelling Cause that will flood their hearts with passion and engage the best that they have within them. Dee Hock, the founder of VISA, put it this way: "All organizations are merely conceptual embodiments of a very old, very basic idea—the idea of community. They can be no more or less than the sum of the beliefs of the people drawn to them; of their character, judgments, acts, and efforts."

"Interesting. I never thought of the company in that way."

"It's true. And what's really lacking in this so-called New Economy of ours where we can work, bank, and even buy groceries online is a deep sense of community. We have lost the essential human connections that are necessary for us to work and live in a state of joy and delight. We have lost that sense of belonging to something larger and more important than ourselves. In the borderless world that has been created by the Internet, what each and every one of us desires is a space and a place where we feel loved, trusted, and significant. A place that we can call 'home.'"

"How do you know so much about the Internet, Julian? You've been secluded in the Himalayas for what seems like an eternity."

"I'm a passionate learner and an obsessive student, Catherine. In this new world we live in, learning no longer ends after we've taken our last exam. It now ends only after we have taken our last breath. Many years ago Erasmus wrote: 'When I get a little money, I buy books; and if any is left, I buy food and clothes.'"

"Wow."

"I'm the same way, little sister. I hunger for knowledge—sometimes I ache for it. While most of what I read and contemplate is from the wisdom literature—the books of the world's greatest thinkers—I do spend time keeping up with what's going on in our world. What good is wisdom if you have no concept of how to apply it in your current circumstances?"

"Good point," I agreed without hesitation. "And so tell me, big brother, what can we do to restore that sense of community in our lives?"

"Great question, Catherine. It's actually the question I was hoping you'd ask. With all the changes in society and within corporations, the sense of community that people once felt has vanished. Loyalty in business is a thing of the past, and restructuring within business has led many workers to believe that it's now a game where every person must fend for themselves if they hope to survive."

"So where are people going to get that sense of community that we all crave?"

"The family," came Julian's speedy reply. "People are retreating into their family lives and making them their highest priority again. People are realizing that they can get all of the social fulfillment they may have once gotten from work within their very own homes. They are realizing that you don't have to leave your front doorstep to get the benefits of being a part of a community—you can get it within the four walls of the very place you live."

"And from the people that love you the most," I added, completely absorbed by what Julian was telling me.

"Right, Catherine. So begin to see your family as your own personal community and the place where most of your personal satisfaction will come from. Understand that through your family, you can gain a richer understanding of yourself and develop greater insight, knowledge, and wisdom. Through your family, you can increase your humanity and actualize your inner strength. The point of wisdom I'm trying to share is simply this: *leadership in your life begins with leadership in your home.* Your family is your foundation, just like the launching pad of a rocket. Once it is secure and in perfect order, you can soar to heights previously unimagined."

"Okay, where's the starting point?"

"It lies in realizing that your family is not all that different from other organizations, BraveLife.com included."

"Really?"

"Really. The parallels are clear. Your company and your family both have unique cultures, don't they?"

"Well, BraveLife.com definitely has its own culture. There are certain ways we dress and certain rules we follow and specific ways we deal with each other that make us unique in comparison with other companies in our field."

"And is your family any different?"

"No, come to think of it, it's not. At home, I guess we do have a culture. We have certain rules, values, and ways of doing things."

"Yes. And like other cultures and organizations, if you want to grow and advance, there's one thing that must be present."

"A dictator?" I asked with a laugh.

"Close, but no cigar, little sister. But I appreciate the humor. The one thing that needs to be present for any family culture to grow into something vibrant and splendid is leadership."

"Leadership? I've never thought that leadership was important in a family or within the home."

"How did BraveLife.com become such an enormous success?" Julian asked. "I mean, I saw your face on the cover of one high-tech magazine in New Delhi!"

"I guess it was primarily because of good management."

"No, it was because of great leadership, Catherine. And by that I don't just mean you and your partners and the rest of the executive team. I mean that *everyone* in the company took a sense of responsibility for and ownership of the company's success. Everyone showed commitment and fidelity to the vision you painted for them. And so your company roared to fortune. The same applies in your home. You must bring leadership into your family and inspire everyone to make a contribution to the culture. You must create a gorgeous future vision of the way you desire things to be for your family and share that Compelling Cause with Jon and the kids. This must be done in a way that excites them and engages their hearts. Only then will your family life reach its highest potential."

"This sounds really far out, Julian, even for you. I mean, Jon is busy with his business and the kids have something on the go constantly. How can I get them to buy into a vision of the ideal family that I wish we could be? And tell me, big brother, how can I get them all to start acting as leaders at home?"

"Easy," came the quick reply. "*You* must show leadership first. As Gandhi said, you must become the change you most wish to see in your life. Lead by example, and I promise you, Jon and the kids will follow."

"Really?"

"Yes. We live in a world where everyone wants everyone else to change first. We blame the government for our problems. We blame our bosses for our stress. We blame the traffic for our misery. But blaming others is merely a convenient way of excusing yourself. Placing the blame for all that's wrong in your life on the shoulders of other people is a nice way to coast through life without ever having to show courage and face your weaknesses head on. It's actually a cowardly way to live and a good way to become a more impotent human being. M. Scott Peck, who wrote *The Road Less Traveled*, put it in these terms: 'Whenever we seek to avoid responsibility for our own behavior, we do so by attempting to give that responsibility to some other individual or organization or entity. But that means that we then give away our power to that entity.'"

Julian's voice was growing louder, and I could see the intensity of his convictions bubbling to the surface. We walked into one of the boardrooms as Julian continued his spirited lesson. "Here's the real message, Catherine.

When you shift the blame and responsibility for something to other people, you are essentially saying that you have no ability to control the problem. You are also saying that you have no choice in the matter and no capacity to influence the outcome. So in blaming other people, you end up giving away your own power, just like Peck says. You are saying 'I can't change things for the better, only they can.' You are in effect saying 'I cannot affect the circumstances of my life, only others can.' And that kind of toxic thinking can send you into a downward spiral that will eventually lead you to a place called nowhere."

"I've never looked at it that way. I recently read that Winston Churchill used to say that 'the price of greatness is responsibility.' Now I know exactly what he meant."

"Look, little sister, what makes us human, at the end of the day, is the power each and every one of us has to choose our response to a specific situation. One person loses their business but sees it as a great life lesson that will make them wiser and better equipped to build an even bigger business. Another, less highly evolved person feels 'road rage' over a big traffic jam. No matter who you are and no matter what your background is, you still have the power to choose how you will process the events of your life. That capacity to choose the way we will interpret what happens to us is our highest human endowment. So don't expect others to change in order for your circumstances to get better. You go ahead and take the noble path. You make the changes that need to be made. I can promise you that the rest of your family will eventually follow."

"Okay," I said, trying to digest all the knowledge Julian was delivering to me as I leaned back in my plush leather chair. "So for me to develop this sense of community at home, I need to be a leader at home?"

"Exactly," replied Julian, looking as out of place in this ultra-modern boardroom as a tulip in a patch of mushrooms as he adjusted the sleeves of his beautiful monk's robe.

"Before I can expect others to change, I must change. Rather than yelling at the kids to be more polite, perhaps I should be more polite to them. Rather than telling them to clean up their rooms so they look tidier, maybe I should organize my home office. And instead of nagging at Jon to start doing things to make our home life more fun and passionate, I guess I should be the one taking the initiative. I should be the one to act as a 'catalyst for change in our family culture,' as you put it ."

"Yup," came Julian's monosyllabic reply. *"The best way to inspire your children to develop into the kind of adults you dream of them becoming is to become the kind of adult you want them to be.* All children, especially young ones like Porter and Sarita, believe that the way their parents act is the correct way to act. You teach them how to act by the way you act. Your values and beliefs become their values and beliefs. Your negative patterns will inevitably become their negative patterns. You need to remember that your children are always watching your every move. And if you think that those little eyes on you are not being influenced in a very profound way by your every word and action, you are just kidding yourself. *Remember, Catherine, after quality time, the second best gift you can give to your kids is the gift of a good example."*

"That's a wonderful insight, Julian."

"You know, I just read a report the other day that I found deeply troubling."

"What did it say?"

"That the average North American child spends approximately five hours a day watching television and just five minutes of quality time with their parents. Too many parents are giving the responsibility of raising their own children to the programming directors of the national networks. And to me, that is a crime."

"What, then, can I do to show family leadership, to really be a leader in my home and build that sense of community that you say we are all craving in this strange new world?"

"The first thing you can do is to open your eyes."

"What do you mean?"

"Helen Keller put it so well when she said 'the most pathetic person in the world is someone who has sight but no vision.' *Too many parents are living day-to-day with no sense of direction in their lives. Rather than living their lives by choice, they live their lives by chance, hoping that everything will work out fine.* But life isn't like that. Living your life by accident, praying things will fall into place and your children will turn out great by default, is about as smart as playing Russian roulette with your life."

"That's a scary thought," I observed, still riveted to Julian's dissertation.

"And I'll tell you, Catherine, if you keep doing the same things each day, you are destined to get the same results each day."

"Someone said the definition of insanity is doing the same things every day and expecting a different result."

"Right. So get in the game and start steering the boat of your family life. Nietzsche made the point well: 'Man's task is simple. He should cease letting his existence be a thoughtless accident.'"

"I'll excuse the gender bias," I noted.

"I will, too, because his lesson is such a good one. If you want to see what your life will look like five years from now, just make certain that you do not change any of your habits, your patterns of thought, or your core beliefs. You will discover that five years from now, you will have a life that is pretty much the same as the one you have today."

"Don't like the sound of that," I replied with complete honesty. "I have much grander dreams for our family's future. I want to have more fun with my kids. I want them to grow stronger, wiser, and more independent. I want Jon and me to become closer and more loving. And I dream of our home becoming a very special place of warmth, growth, and joy that offers us all a sanctuary from the harshness of the world we now live in."

"Well, then, Catherine, please understand that for your family life to improve, the way you view the world must first improve. You must create a compelling vision on the picture screen of your imagination about what you want your family culture to look like. You must then clarify that ideal in your mind so it is vivid and strikingly precise. Finally, you must commit it to paper."

"Why?"

"Because when you commit the vision you have for your family's future to paper, it becomes an agreement."

"Really?" I wondered.

"Definitely," responded my brother. "It becomes like a pledge or a binding contract that you have made with yourself. Your beliefs in life are really nothing more than agreements you have made with yourself about the state of affairs you find yourself in. Some people believe they are too busy to hug their children many times a day to show them their love. In doing so, they have made an agreement with themselves in an effort to justify that 'fact.' Some people believe that they can never live great lives because their pasts have been too difficult. In doing so, they have made an agreement with themselves and resigned themselves to live by that 'fact'. The agreements you make with yourself are extremely powerful, Catherine."

"I've never thought about our beliefs in this way, Julian."

"So here's what I want you to do. You know what you want for your family life, and now you have committed yourself to doing what it takes to get there."

"Correct."

"Now create a Family Vision Agreement that will then serve as your daily guide so that you can make wiser choices about how you will spend your days and invest your time. It will serve as a commitment statement that will keep you focused on The Things That Truly Count."

"So by developing this Family Vision Agreement and translating it into writing, I will stop living by chance and start living by choice?" I asked, genuinely fascinated by the strategy Julian was revealing to me.

"Yes. You will finally be in control of your destiny. Your Family Vision Agreement will serve as your lighthouse, always guiding you 'home'—to that place of love and peace—no matter how rough the seas become. It will give you hope and an overwhelming sense of promise for better things to come. And it will protect you and your family."

"Protect us?"

"Yes. Knowing exactly what you want for the future of your family protects you from all those negative influences that try and creep into our lives. When your thoughts are crystal clear and you are completely committed to your vision of your family's future, then the opinions of others mean nothing. The hypnotic pull of the ads on television dictating what the ideal family should look like has no hold over you. The need to keep up with the neighbors and your colleagues falls to the wayside. You and your family become *independent*. And, in so doing, you are elevated to a much wiser, more enlightened way of leading your family life."

"I'd love for the kids to be independent, Julian. I've learned that independent thinking is a key factor in business success. Colin Baden, the VP of Design at Oakley Sunglasses, was recently quoted in *Fast Company* magazine—"

"Oooh, I love that publication," Julian interjected.

"You read *Fast Company?*" I replied in surprise.

"Told you I'm hungry for knowledge. It's a great read."

"Well, anyway," I went on, "this senior executive was quoted as saying, 'If you're doing something a certain way because it's always been done that way, then you're probably doing it the wrong way.' I loved that because it strikes at the heart of why we need to be independent thinkers if we hope to excel in business these days."

"And in life these days. So have the courage to create your Family Vision Agreement so you can begin doing things your way, according to what your heart..."

"And Jon's heart," I interrupted quickly.

"And Jon's heart," Julian corrected, "tells you is morally correct. And putting that vision of what you want your family life to look like in the future into a concrete form is also one of the best ways I know of to increase your level of commitment to your family."

"Why?"

"Because I have discovered in my own life that *the things that get committed to paper are the things that are committed to in life.*"

"I agree," I replied excitedly. "One of the secrets to the success I've experienced in my professional life was insisting on great clarity about what results I wanted. I used to write down my career goals for every ninety days and read them almost daily to maintain my focus and to help me seize opportunities that might pass through my days undetected."

"Nicely said, Catherine. Do the same in your family life. I suggest you take the Family Vision Agreement, study it closely, prioritize what is most important, and then create goals—with deadlines around each priority."

"That's the kind of strategic thinking that made us so successful in BraveLife.com."

"And it's the kind of strategic thinking that will now make you even more successful in your home life. I cannot understand why people meticulously plan their professional lives but give no attention at all to the way they will live at home." Julian paused and grew more reflective as his fingers played with a brass coaster on the table. He looked down for a few seconds and then spoke again. "Great leaders are more thoughtful than others, Catherine. They take the time to go into seclusion every once in a while to do nothing but think. Einstein used to do that, you know?"

"I wasn't aware of that," I confessed.

"Yes, I read he had a special 'thinking chair' that he would retreat to in a silent place. And once in it, he would do nothing but think."

"Our best salesperson does the same thing," I said. "He blocks off one day every other week to 'get lost' as he calls it. He leaves his pager and his cellphone in the office and goes off to a place where no one can reach him. All he takes with him is a legal-sized notepad and a pencil. And all he does for that whole day is think."

"I'm impressed," replied Julian, nodding his head with a gentle smile. "I think I'd like the guy."

"We all thought he was crazy. Until we saw the results. His sales were five times higher than his nearest competitor. Five times higher! So one day I sat him down to figure out his process. He told me that during that 'Strategy Day,' as he called it, he'd think about his future and what he dreamed it would look like. He wrote things down so they became clearer and clearer in his mind."

"See, *clarity precedes mastery*," Julian interjected gleefully.

"Well, it sure did in his case," I continued. "He told me that the more time he spent in solitude, just thinking about and defining what he wanted out of life, the more ideas his imagination would deliver to him. And as these brainstorms came, he just kept writing them all down with his pencil. The entire scope of his consciousness became concentrated around his highest priorities. He dreamed, thought, and spoke of little else. He then built specific goals around these objectives and added deadlines for the accomplishment of each one. He told me that these special days filled him with so much hope and energy he could barely contain himself. And with this renewed focus, he would come back to the office and dazzle us all once again."

Julian then did something that left me speechless. He quickly rose to his feet and then jumped up onto the gleaming meeting table. Then he started to dance, mildly at first, and then wildly, as if he had entered some sort of a trance.

"Julian! What are you doing? Have you lost your mind! Please stop that right now. I'm getting scared. Please stop that," I pleaded, alarmed at what I was seeing.

"Not to worry, little sista," replied Julian, mocking the style of those millionaire rap stars who dominate the record charts. "Just havin' some fun."

"C'mon, Julian. These are the corporate offices of a multibillion-dollar firm. You need to exercise some restraint in here."

"'Each day, and the living of it, has to be a conscious creation in which discipline and order are relieved with some play and pure foolishness,'" came his cryptic reply.

"What?"

"Those are the words of May Sarton. And I live by them. I live my life with great discipline and virtue, but I ensure that I make time for fun while I'm at it. So c'mon up here with me and join me in my little dance. There's a point I'm trying to make."

I reflected on Julian's unusual request. I'll agree that my brother's behavior was eccentric. But there was no longer any doubt in my mind that the wisdom Julian had connected with in those mountains had given him insights that had the power to transform my life, if I only had the courage to embrace them. Julian had developed an uncanny ability to teach me precisely the lessons I needed to learn to move forward, and I realized that if I refused to listen to him, I would be the one to suffer, not him.

"Okay. You win," I said, reluctantly climbing up onto the meeting table with him, my shoes still on.

"Now dance!" laughed Julian. "Let the little child in you see the light of day. She's been begging to come out and play. It'll be good for your soul."

I moved my feet a little but felt too self-conscious to do much more.

"Dance, or I'll start singing, Catherine," Julian threatened with a smile that made his eyes twinkle.

"Oh, all right," I replied, as I started to wave my hands in the air, mimicking John Travolta in *Saturday Night Fever* and starting to feel pretty good in the process. "Hey, this is kind of fun, Julian," I added, shaking my body from side to side.

"I know it is. Never be too busy to dance, little sista!" he yelled, pumping both his bronzed fists in the air and whirling around in a remarkable display of athletic prowess.

Just then my senior vice president walked past the boardoom. A few seconds later he returned, his eyes bulging and his face conveying total surprise. He just stared at the two of us up on the boardroom table. I immediately came to a standstill. Julian continued his wild dance with delight. I think he enjoyed the fact that we had been caught. My colleague remained frozen in his tracks, observing this odd scene through the glass wall that separated us. Then he started to laugh. He popped his head into the boardroom.

"Nice to see you've fully recovered, Catherine. When you have time, you'll have to share that new management practice you've discovered with the rest of the executive team," he joked.

"I will, Les, I promise I will," I responded, grateful for his indulgence of my peculiar behavior.

After the VP left, I looked at Julian.

"Julian, what's the point here? I'll be the laughingstock of this whole company if I keep doing this kind of thing."

"Okay, Catherine. I was just having some fun with you. But back to my teaching. Here's the point. Standing on this table allows you to gain a new perspective. It allows you to see things from a higher place. Remember the astronauts and their lunar landing?"

"Of course."

"Well, when they came back, they mentioned repeatedly how being up there and looking down on the earth gave them a completely new perspective on our world. Even more important, they said this higher view of our planet gave them a wiser understanding of life on it."

"So standing up on this table allows me to see the world in a better way?" I asked, a little confused at the metaphor Julian was offering.

"It gets back to the Family Vision Agreement I've been talking about. In the same way that getting up on this meeting table allows you to take a broader view of your offices, creating your Family Vision Agreement will allow you to keep a broader perspective on your life. You will always be able to keep the big picture in mind rather than getting sucked down into the mundane distractions that keep us from experiencing the happiness and pleasure of this gift we call life. You will always have an aerial view of the tiny community you love as your family. You will no longer spend your days majoring in minor things. Instead, you will be in a position to concentrate your time on the Vital Few."

"The Vital Few?" I asked, not having come across this term before.

"Yes, The Vital Few. Being a great leader, in your company, and even more important in your home, means you need to focus on The Vital Few rather than on the Mundane Many. Most people spend the best years of their lives consumed by activities that do not advance them in the direction of their ideal life. They watch too much television, think constantly about what's wrong in their lives rather than what's right, gossip on the telephone, and criticize their kids. The Family Vision Agreement will help you stay centered on those few meaningful activities that yield the greatest positive results in your life and ensure that you end up exactly where you dream of ending."

Julian got down from the table and leaned against the wall, pausing for dramatic effect.

"Writing down your Family Vision Agreement and specific goals to enrich your home culture will do just that: you will be able to detect opportunities to build a greater family that you would have otherwise missed because you were not looking for them. *See, what you focus on in your life grows and what you think about expands. And the things you invest your attention in grow in importance.*"

"I agree that what you focus on grows. I find that when I get a new client, the next day I'll be driving around the city and I see signs of that new client everywhere. I might see one of their trucks with their logo on it drive past me on the freeway or I'll notice their advertisement in the paper or I'll see their head office as I make my way home. All these things were there before, I just failed to detect them until they came into the scope of my focus. And then I see them everywhere."

"It's a powerful observation and something that I think we all experience on a regular basis. Once you start paying attention to something, it expands into your consciousness and floods into your awareness. That's why I always say that *awareness precedes change*. Before you can change something in your life, you must first become aware of it and begin to really pay attention to it. You must build some awareness around it. You will never be able to eliminate a weakness you don't even know about."

"Just so I understand, you are saying that setting my Family Vision Agreement onto paper so it becomes a true agreement, and then breaking it down into specific goals, will cause me to pay more attention to these things in my life."

"Yes."

"And are you also saying that this act will allow me to see all those opportunities to build a better home life that most of us busy parents never even notice because our energy is taken up by all the little emergencies that seem to occupy every waking minute?"

"Exactly. It reminds me of that Hollywood screen-writer I used to have drinks with."

"I remember him well. He used to wear cowboy boots and never went anywhere without a bottle of Evian water in his hand."

"That's him. He once told me that the secret of his success in Hollywood was that *he always wrote the endings first*. He created the perfect ending and then worked his way backwards."

"Brilliant."

"I agree. And that's what I'm suggesting you do in your family life. Close your eyes and picture the happiest ending you could possibly imagine. Then work your way backwards until today. See, the Family Vision Agreement is really the story of your life—as it relates to your family. In defining it and committing it to written form, you will be able to make smart choices about how you spend every minute of any day. If an activity or behavior does not somehow advance you along the script you have envisioned—towards that happy ending—you simply don't do it."

"Got it," I replied, finally grasping the importance of the concept. "Did the Sages of Sivana teach you all this knowledge?"

"They taught me the organizing principles for a great life. They taught me that loving relationships form the foundation of a life greatly lived. They taught me that our thoughts form our world and that to improve our lives we must first improve our thinking. And they taught me so much more. For many months after I left their tiny

Himalayan village, I thought about all the lessons these very special human beings shared with me. I built upon their teachings and then forged my own insights on what it takes to live our best lives. I came up with ideas that even I am surprised I arrived at. And those insights are what I'm sharing with you, my dear sister."

"Sista, for short," I said with a wink. Julian giggled.

"But Julian, what else can I do to show real leadership at home and foster that sense of community with the family?"

"Make your home a haven," came the simple reply.

"Can you elaborate on that a little for me, big brother?"

"In Sivana, high up in those Himalayan mountains, the sages always treasured their homes. Even though they lived in the most peaceful and serene place I've ever seen, those little huts that they lived in were their real sanctuaries. They made sure that their simple little homes were always clean and full of sunlight. They were always careful to ensure that fresh air filled their living spaces and flowers were everywhere. And they took pains to make certain that while they often invited one another over to discuss philosophy and share wisdom, their homes offered plenty of time for silent reflection, introspection, and self-examination. What I'm saying is that in this noisy, bustling world we find ourselves in, you can show some real family leadership by making sure that your home becomes a haven for you, Jon, and the kids."

"And for you too, Julian. We love having you live with us. Even though you appear so youthful, Porter and Sarita sense your wisdom and your age. They are absolutely thrilled to have you in our home and have come to see you as the grandfather they never had."

"Gee, thanks," replied Julian.

"It's funny—you have such a calming influence on them. Jon and I are always telling them to hurry up, and you are always reminding them to slow down."

"Grandparents are like that, aren't they? Throughout our civilization, all families have revered their elders and sat at their feet to learn life's most important lessons. In the Himalayas, extended families were the norm. The sages wouldn't think of living in a place without their mothers and fathers being around. Their elders were a constant source of comfort, knowledge, and love."

"And I'll bet the young monks benefited the most."

"Yes, they did. And even here in the West, ask school-teachers if they can tell which of their young students have had the influence of grandparents in their lives, and they will always reply in the affirmative. They are the kids who are calmer, quieter, and more trusting of other human beings. They are the kids who are more independent, thoughtful, and compassionate. Look at our own family's experience, Catherine, with Grandpa and Grandma Mantle. They always gave me that feeling that life would turn out right in the end."

"They did, Julian. I really miss them."

"Me, too. I'm delighted that the kids love having me around. I love them deeply. I feel such joy when Porter sits on my knee and Sarita cuddles in my arms, and they ask me to tell them stories about my adventures in India. And I'm finding that they teach me as much as I teach them. The sages believed that children come to us more highly evolved than adults to teach us the lessons we need to learn. Porter and Sarita certainly do that. They remind me of the importance of staying playful, of being curious, and of being consistently compassionate every day. Makes me think of the words of the ancient philosopher Heraclitus who observed: 'Man is most nearly himself when he achieves the seriousness of a child at play.'"

"Not that you need your spirits lifted, Julian. You are always so positive. I think you are really comfortable in your new skin. And I couldn't be happier for you."

"Thanks. Helen Keller, a woman I greatly admire, once said: 'No pessimist ever discovered the secrets of the stars, or sailed to an uncharted land, or opened a new heaven to the human spirit.'"

"Lovely words."

"They are, aren't they? When I was practicing law, I laughed at people who talked about positive thinking and read self-help books. I'd smile with a sense of superiority when I'd see people rushing to the subway after work clutching books with odd titles such as *MegaLiving!* and *Who Will Cry When You Die? Why would you read a self-help book if you were normal?* was what I would think back then. But my thinking has evolved. I've come to understand, through my time with those great sages, that the most normal and wise thing you can do as a person is work on yourself. The best possible use of your time, bar none, lies in cultivating your mind, character, and spirit so that you can be more to this world. Buddha said it best: 'Carpenters bend wood. Fletchers bend arrows. And wise people fashion themselves.'"

"When I was putting a new bouquet of flowers in your room like you asked me to, I saw all those quotes you have pasted to the ceiling."

"Pretty cool, huh?" remarked Julian proudly. "At night, after the kids are in bed, I go up to my room, lie in bed, and recite each and every one of those quotes out loud. It deepens my commitment to living by the timeless success principles that have governed humanity."

"I loved the ancient Indian one that read: 'There is nothing noble about being superior to others. True nobility lies in being superior to your former self,'" I noted reflectively.

"Those are compelling words, aren't they? They strike at the core of what the purpose of life really entails. It's not about competing against others. It's about winning against yourself, growing as a person each day, and making yourself a more valuable human being."

"So we can add more value to all those around us."

"You got it, Catherine," affirmed Julian, clearly pleased with my correct response. "Now back to what I was saying about making your home a haven."

"I'm eager to work on this one."

"I recommend that you begin by filling your home with great books. Teach Porter and Sarita that *to lead in their lives they must read in their days*. One of the finest gifts a parent can give their children is a love of reading, a passion for good books. All the answers to any question the kids might ever have in their lives are contained within books. Through the discipline of daily reading, Porter and Sarita can spend time with the greatest people who have ever graced the planet. They can get deep into the minds of history's wisest thinkers and learn their most intimate insights. I recommend you schedule a thirty-minute reading session every night with your children. Get them hooked on a special author or on a fascinating series so that they look forward to this time. I promise you this simple nightly ritual will influence their lives in such a positive way."

"Wonderful idea, Julian. I guess I just assumed they would learn all this stuff in school."

"Schools only supplement the teachings of parents. In this day and age, where parents have too much to do in too little time, it's easy to sit back and hope that the school teaches your children all the things you would have taught them if you weren't so busy trying to do all the things that are competing for your attention. But that's the wrong approach. Showing leadership as a parent means doing all those things that your conscience tells you are the right things to do, even though they might not be the easy things to do."

"Any examples?" I asked, intrigued.

"Sure. After a long day of work, you might just want to do nothing more than watch TV on the couch. But say Sarita wants you to read to her. The easy thing to do would be to brush her off and get Jon to take her out for a walk. But the right thing to do would be to turn off the television, pick up a book, and read to your daughter. Doing that is showing great leadership within your home."

"True," I agreed.

"Another example might involve speaking your truth with Porter."

"Speaking my truth? What does that mean?"

"Speaking your truth means speaking from your heart. Far too many people in our world speak only in the words they know the people around them want to hear. They use their words to manipulate and control rather than to express their true feelings and build the kind of understanding that always leads to greater love. In using words that do not reflect what they really mean or how they truly feel, they live their lives in a state of spiritual dishonesty. Only by speaking your truth—what you truly feel, believe and know—will you be in a position to be the family leader that you are destined to be."

"Wow," was the only reply that I could muster.

"Now back to the example. All too often in life, we run away from our fears. Wise, enlightened, and fully evolved people make a point of running *toward* their fears. Most of us hate confronting people over things we perceive they have done to us that have made us feel bad. Someone puts us down or treats us poorly and rather than having the courage to raise the issue in a mature way, we pretend it never happened. But the problem with that is that the wound festers."

"And it drains your energy, too," I added.

"Exactly, Catherine. And so all these little wounds add up to an enormous weight that you end up carrying around with you on the journey of life. Showing leadership means you deal with issues as they come up, in a mature, rational, and heartfelt way, no matter how uncomfortable it is for you to confront them head on. So let's say that when Porter gets a little older—perhaps into his early teen years—he does something that embarrasses you. You have a choice: you can run from the issue or you can deal with the issue. Running from it guarantees that the wound will fester. Dealing with it means that Porter will gain some awareness of his actions and that greater understanding will evolve between the two of you."

"So leadership is, in many ways, about taking the high road and making the tough choice—no matter how uncomfortable it makes me feel."

"Yes. And I'll tell you what. *The tougher you are with yourself, the easier life will be on you. The stricter you are with yourself, the gentler life will be on you.*"

"What do you mean?"

"I mean that when you get stricter with yourself and rein in all those weaker impulses and have the self-discipline to do what's right—every time—your life is certain to turn out great. *Deferring what is easy to do and preferring those activities that your heart tells you are the right ones always leads you to the family life of your dreams.*"

"The one I will have defined in my Family Vision Agreement?"

"Precisely, little sister. Precisely."

In a grand, sweeping gesture, Julian reached over and pulled the hood of his robe over his head. He looked out of the window and he scanned the horizon, which was filled with skyscrapers containing many thousands of people struggling with the same issues I was dealing with.

"I've got to get going, Catherine. I've got a meeting with someone."

"Might I ask with whom?" I blurted out, burning with curiosity.

"I have to meet a craftsperson. He's working on a special project for me. You will know about it when the time is right," was all Julian would reveal. "But let me finish up this lesson before I go. So what I was saying is: take responsibility for your children's moral development. Don't expect the kids' school to do everything. That's not fair to the kids or to the school. And give Porter and Sarita a great love of great books. Henry David Thoreau referred to these as the 'heroic books' in his classic work *Walden*, books that he said contained the noblest recorded thoughts of humankind."

"But Sarita can't read and Porter is just getting into *Arthur* and *Curious George* books. Does it really make sense to fill our home with great biographies and the wise books of philosophers when he cannot really read?"

"He might not be able to read on his own, but you can certainly read to him. If you are serious about inspiring your children to become great leaders in their own lives, then you must expose them to the lives of other great people who lived before them. As I mentioned, few things are as powerful to kids as good examples. If you want your children to love learning, turn off the television and read for an hour a night yourself. If you want your children to commit themselves to excellence, make sure you do the same. By filling your home with great books and making the time to read them—even for fifteen minutes a day—you will send a powerful message to your children that *reading matters*. As well, I can think of no better legacy to leave to your wonderful children than a library containing the thoughts of the wisest people who have ever graced the earth. Knowing Porter and Sarita, they will thank you for it forever."

"What an incredible idea, Julian. Building a library of the world's greatest books for my children as a tribute to them."

"It would be a wonderful thing to do, Catherine. So wherever you go, keep hunting for special books to add to their collection. Read aloud from these books nightly. You may think they will not understand them, but the wisdom they receive will be tucked away deep in their minds. And those seeds that you plant within their characters will eventually sprout into the great acts of enlightened adults," noted Julian poetically.

"When we were growing BraveLife.com, we brought in some consultants who coached us to create a learning culture at work. They told us that if we really wanted to have productive and creative employees, it was our duty as the leaders of that organization to foster an environment where people loved to learn."

"Fair point. We now live in a world where ideas are the commodity of success. In the old economy, value was defined by bricks and brawn—how many offices you owned and how many employees you had. In the new economy, organizational success is defined by the brains and beliefs, the quality of the ideas your people generate. One idea, coming from one person's mind, can transform the world. And if you don't believe me, just think about Bill Gates or Steve Jobs, to use but two examples from the high-tech field you work within. Their ideas about the potential of computers have changed the way we live. One idea, if acted upon with great intensity and relentless commitment, really can change the world."

"And it's not just in business," I added. "Nelson Mandela started out with nothing more than the simple idea that his people deserved to be free."

"As did Mahatma Gandhi."

"Amelia Earhart had a simple idea about aviation."

"Another good example," affirmed Julian.

"And Einstein's ideas transformed science."

"Correct, little sister. The greatest leaders in this new world will be the greatest thinkers. So your duty as a parent is to listen to those high-priced consultants you brought in and *create a learning culture*—not only in your company but also within your home. Make learning fun. Make your house a playground of ideas where the kids are truly passionate about learning. Model Curious George!"

"Model Curious George?" I asked in surprise.

"Porter and Sarita love Curious George, right?"

"He's their hero," I replied.

"Well, every Curious George book starts off with the same sentence. Do you remember it?"

"Sure: 'George was a good little monkey, but he was always very curious.'"

"Right. What I'm saying to you is that your duty as a parent is to instill a burning sense of curiosity within Porter and Sarita. Teach them to be hungry for knowledge and thirsty for wisdom. Coach them to love books and music and ideas. This is how they will succeed in this world of boundless change."

"Anything else I can do to make our home a haven after I've created what you call 'a learning culture' for the family?"

"Flowers," came the reply. "For about $3.49, you can walk out of any grocery store with a bouquet of flowers that will have a million-dollar effect on your home environment."

"Really?"

"The simple act of placing even a bouquet or two of flowers in your home can flood it with a feeling of peace and tranquility. In Sivana, the sages filled their tiny homes with flowers and worshiped them as symbols of all that is good about life. Flowers in your home will add color, they will keep you connected to the simple pleasures of life, and they will teach the kids that nature is a positive force in our lives."

"I agree, Julian. Since I've been home, I've started going for weekly walks in the woods, in the same woods we used to play in as children. I've also started unplugging the television while the kids are watching it and taking them out into the woods with me as often as I can. We collect leaves. We play hide and seek. And we skip rocks on that big pond you used to go skinny dipping in."

Julian squealed with laughter. "I remember. We had some glorious times as kids, didn't we?"

"We sure did. But you're absolutely right. The time the kids and I spend in natural surroundings is so special for us. It really bonds us and brings out the best in our hearts. And I know it does wonders for their creativity."

"My advice is to try and do as much as you can to make the inside of your home beautiful. Develop an intense appreciation for beauty. Increase your awareness of what is beautiful. As this awareness grows, let's say through the strategic use of flowers throughout your house, you will discover you begin to notice even more beauty in your home—and in your life."

"The mind is an incredible thing, isn't it, Julian?"

"That it is. And the sages taught me so much about its workings and its wonders." Julian pressed on without missing a beat. "To make your home a haven, I also suggest that you adopt another of the rituals of the sages and let fresh air pass through every room in the house."

"Why?"

"It's one of those ancient Eastern habits that even now I don't fully understand. But Catherine, I encourage you to judge by results and by results alone. My little room always has the windows open, and I know it is one of the reasons for my high energy level and excellent health. Perhaps it's because the more oxygen we allow to enter our lungs, the greater our personal vitality will be. The sages used to say that 'to breathe properly is to live properly.' In my own life, I make certain that I breathe fresh air daily. On my morning walks, I breathe consciously and deeply and completely. This simple discipline fills my body with vitality and a radiant energy. What's the first thing we do after we are born, Catherine?"

"We breathe air into ourselves."

"Correct. So please remember that proper breathing practice is central to life."

"Okay, anything else to make my home a special sanctuary that will build our family culture and help us get to where we dream of getting?"

"Three final suggestions before I go. First, let lots of sunlight into your home. It really does warm the soul and make things most pleasant. Again, look at my living quarters. I put a skylight in for this very purpose, and the rays of the sun keep me smiling throughout the day. Second, try and have quiet family time—especially in the evenings when Jon is back from work and the kids are home from school. Most parents give no thought to the amount of noise in their home environments, and yet this is one of the most important factors in the development of a peaceful mind-set. *Your environment shapes your thinking.* If the television is always on, the video games are always running, and the radio is always blaring, your home will never be an oasis of peace—a haven—from the outside world. To really create a sanctuary that your whole family will love to spend time within, make certain it is a calm place to be."

"Sounds so good when you describe it," I said eagerly.

"Give your kids an appreciation of solitude. As they get older, show them that there is no need for them to constantly have the radio playing, the computer humming, and the phones ringing. Encourage them to enjoy stimulating conversation. Suggest that they cultivate the habit of letter writing. And inspire them to watch beautiful sunsets and dream big dreams."

"I'd love for the kids to love those things," I replied wistfully.

"A wonderful ritual to incorporate into your family culture is a daily meal where the whole family sits down together to enjoy each other's company. Many years ago, the family mealtime was a cherished part of nearly every family's routine. But sadly, with all the demands that have now been placed upon our time, this habit has been lost. I suggest that you use this sacred time to ask about each other's day and what each family member learned from it. Talk about your Family Vision Agreement or other important things that you wish to share. Share a new point of interest or a funny story you might have heard. The main point is to see this as an excellent opportunity to reconnect at the end of the day. Oh, and make certain that you turn off all the phones during this family meal so you will never be interrupted."

"I guess that's what voicemail is for, isn't it?"

"True."

"And yet we all seem to have this urge to run and pick up the phone every time it rings, even if we are doing something important with the kids."

Julian nodded and then continued. I sensed that he was anxious to leave, but wanted to share as much wisdom as he could with me before doing so.

"Implementing the strategy of a daily family mealtime is a fabulous way to show real leadership at home. *And remember, as a parent you are a leader. Leadership is not the sole domain of the CEO. Whether you work in a boardroom such as this or within your home as a full-time parent, you are a leader.*"

"And the final point?"

"*Never forget that the family that plays together is the family that stays together.* Every few weeks, have a Laughter Night where you rent funny movies from the video store or do silly things at home guaranteed to make everyone laugh. Never lose that fabulous sense of humor you have, Catherine. And teach your children the power of a good belly laugh. Laughter truly is the shortest distance between people and one of the wisest ways to deepen your human connections. Life can be difficult at times, but keep your perspective and make the time to laugh together on a regular basis. The more you laugh, the more Porter and Sarita will see that being an adult is actually not such a serious occupation after all. Have you watched the kids when they pretend they are you and Jon?"

"Yes, I have."

"Well, they grow so serious, don't they?"

"You're right, they do," I answered, shuddering at this realization.

"Do they laugh and giggle when they are imitating the two of you?"

"Nope," I responded quietly.

"So what I said earlier might just be true. Children do come to us more highly evolved than adults to teach us the lessons we need to learn. And perhaps, my great little sister who I love so much, the lesson for you is to lighten up."

"But I did dance on this table," I laughed.

"You did," replied Julian, giving me a big hug and then his trademark kiss on my forehead. "I know you are all going to have great lives, and your children will mature into fine teenagers and excellent adults. You need not have any worries about that. Take all I have taught you this morning to heart. Reflect on the wisdom I've shared for the rest of the day and think deeply of how you can integrate it all to create a rich family culture and a home that is your special community of love. Your life will move from the cocoon of the ordinary into the realm of the extraordinary."

And with that, my brother, the great Julian Mantle, turned and dashed off, leaving me alone in the board-room as the rays of a glorious afternoon bathed me in light. I felt so happy about what I had learned that morning that I felt like dancing on the table.

The Second Mastery of the Family Leader™

Shift from Scolding the Child to Molding the Leader

"Make it a rule never if possible to lie down at night without being able to say, 'I have made one human being at least a little wiser, a little happier or a little better this day.'"
—Charles Kingsley

"I had not loved enough. I'd been busy, busy, so busy, preparing for life, while life floated by me, quiet and swift as a regatta."
—Lorene Cary

JULIAN'S ADVICE THAT THE FAMILY was an organization that required leadership like all other organizations was not lost on me. In the weeks following our remarkable meeting downtown at the BraveLife.com offices, I set about making some profound changes in the way we did things at home. Jon and I came to see ourselves as leaders and catalysts of change. We recognized that Julian was right: *parents are leaders* and we had to stop doing what was easy in our lives and start doing what was right. The two of us went on many long walks while Julian played with Porter and Sarita, and we started to carve out the beginnings of our Family Vision Agreement, a contract that we both promised would guide our actions. We analyzed what kind of examples we were setting for our children by the way we were conducting our lives and wrote out a long list of all the things we knew we had to improve.

Many hundreds of years ago, Thomas Fuller wrote: "He does not believe who does not live according to his belief." To me, that means that if you don't live by the values that you profess to believe in, then you don't really believe in them. Say what you want, but talk is cheap and *the evidence never lies.* You can tell the world that your family comes first, but if you miss family dinners for business meetings most days of the week, the fact of the matter is that your family really does not come first. You can preach the power of reading and offer your children good books, but if you spend most of your free time watching sitcoms on TV, then you really don't believe that learning is the priority you say it is. After the plane crash, there was no doubt in my mind that my family was the most important priority in my world. Now I had to live that value.

Those early days after the crash, with Julian living with us up in that simple room above the garage, were precious times. Jon and I grew closer with each passing day. The more we discussed how we could improve our family culture and make our home a haven, the more we rekindled that spark of caring that we both thought we'd lost. I came to develop a greater appreciation for the strength of Jon's character and for the man that he was. In turn, Jon told me that he honored me for my intellect, my self-discipline, and my new passion for life. We grew to understand each other more. We came to respect each other more. And we came to love each other more than we ever had in the past.

Rebuilding my relationship with the children and Jon was not always easy, though. Yes, we made tremendous progress in a relatively short period of time, in large part because of the strength of my commitment to improve our family life. But after so many years of neglect on my part, challenges were bound to occur.

Jon sometimes felt bitter over the lost years and the special family times I had missed. Since he was not the most vocal of people, this frustration was often masked in apathy. He would tell me he was not interested in going for a picnic or trying a new dish I wanted the two of us to cook together. That great leader of human beings Mahatma Gandhi once said that "three-fourths of the miseries and misunderstandings in the world will disappear if we step into the shoes of our adversaries and understand their standpoint." While Jon was clearly not my adversary, I often relied on this phrase to help me when things grew trying with him. I'd ask myself, "What must he be feeling right now, and how can I help him through it?" I really tried to "get behind his eyeballs" and view things from his perspective. Each one of us sees the world through our own stained-glass window, each color of that window representing an experience, attitude, or bias. It was helpful to view the world through his.

With time, I came to realize that it was more than just time together that Jon needed. He craved greater understanding. He wanted to be loved deeply and have a partner whom he could love completely in return. He wanted someone who would celebrate the little victories he won as he built his own business, and someone to whom he could open up when the cards did not fall in quite the way he had hoped. He wanted a partner he could laugh with, a lover he could learn from, and a wife who would become his best friend all over again.

I'll also come clean and admit that Porter and Sarita did not always cooperate either. Of course, they were thrilled that I spent so much time with them and that I had moved my office into our home. They loved the fact that I was less serious, more playful, and far more affectionate with them than I'd ever been. But all that time away from them did take its toll. They sometimes became clingy and wouldn't leave my side. At other times, they threw tantrums over issues that other kids might have not given a second thought to. I sensed that their insecurity lay in the fact that they never knew when this newly created dream might end and their mother might get called back into work to resume her former lifestyle. I also realized that it would take some time for me to fully regain Porter and Sarita's trust. A few months of being the ideal parent is no substitute for a lifetime of commitment and dedication to one's children.

I realized that my vision of becoming an excellent parent was a work-in-progress. I learned to be gentle with myself and to accept my past failings with grace. They were a necessary part of my evolution, I came to understand. "Everything happens for a reason," I would remind myself. The unfolding of every life is a process. We live, we falter, and then we learn and grow. I simply promised myself I would accept Julian's wisdom with an open heart and apply his ideas with a gentle faith. I felt certain that the results would come and my best life would eventually reveal itself.

After many late-night discussions and much intro-spection on our parts, Jon and I both began to take a far greater sense of responsibility for what went on within our home. As more time passed, the residual apathy that

Jon showed from time to time melted into sympathy and an appreciation of how hard I was working to get our family culture to the place where we both knew it could be. We started laughing more often and since laughter is contagious, the kids soon came to follow our lead. We all started hugging each other many times a day, and saying "I love you" became as common in our home as spilled milk and Saturday-morning cartoons. And we all began to really enjoy doing nothing more than being in each other's company.

Just so you know exactly how we got our transformation going after that meeting with Julian downtown, the first thing Jon and I did was to formulate the Family Vision Agreement that Julian had encouraged us to develop. It made perfect sense to us: it would be impossible to hit a target we could not see. If we really wanted to make wholesale improvements in our family life and make our home culture one based on deep love and happiness, we had to have a clear picture of the end result in our minds and then articulate it on paper. "Clarity precedes mastery" was the phrase Julian kept on repeating to the both of us while we all relaxed in the family room.

By clarifying our future, defining our values, and reflecting upon our priorities, we began living in a much more intentional and deliberate way. Life no longer acted on us—we took charge of our lives and lived out our days on our own terms. Personally, I felt more peaceful and in control. That sense of being over-whelmed, which dominates the lives of most of us in this wild and woolly world where we juggle full-time jobs with grocery shopping, soccer practices and volunteer work, began to subside. Life became fun again.

As for Julian, he spent most of his days reading and meditating in his neat little room above the garage. From time to time I'd hear banging and sawing, but I pretty much stopped going up there in a bid to give Julian the freedom I knew he needed. Sometimes he'd come into our family room covered in sawdust, muttering some-thing about "those darned craftspeople. I hope they know what they're doing." I didn't ask what he meant.

Julian's needs were few: fresh flowers whenever I had time to pick them up for him, lots of fresh air, and plenty of time with Porter and Sarita. His love for them grew profound as the weeks rolled along. Julian had been a good father to Ally over the course of her all-too-brief life. But with his newfound wisdom and compassion, I sensed he would be a great parent if he ever decided to have chil-dren again. One morning I asked him about this.

"Hi, Julian," I said as he walked in the side door, a bottle of spring water in his hand after his customary morning walk.

"Good morning, Catherine. I think it's going to be one brilliant day out there. Did you see the way the moon is still visible in the sky even though the sun is blazing?"

"I hadn't noticed. But I'll have a peek once I drop Porter off at school and Sarita off at Jon's mom's place. She's been away on vacation and wants to spend the day doing arts and crafts with her granddaughter. She's such a nice woman, Julian."

"So I've heard. Mind if I tag along with you in the car?"

"Sure, that would be great. Sarita loves it when you sit in the back seat with her and do your hilarious 'tour guide' routine."

"I'll do anything to amuse her," replied Julian.

"I know."

After we dropped the kids off, I started asking Julian some of the questions that had been on my mind.

"Julian?"

"Yes, Catherine."

"Do you think you will ever get married again?"

"What?" exclaimed Julian, breaking into laughter.

"No, I'm serious. You look phenomenal. You are the wisest person I've ever met. You are so fun to be around, and you have the most positive attitude I could ever imagine. I think there would be many opportunities for you to meet someone special. Maybe even have another child."

Julian looked out of the passenger window and fell completely silent. I didn't say another word. Soon, his eyes welled up with tears that then gathered and drizzled down his smooth cheeks, ending up on the folds of his ever-present red robe.

"Sorry, Julian. I didn't mean to bring back bad memories," I apologized.

"You actually brought back good ones," Julian answered sweetly. "My days with Ally were the best days of my life. Having Porter and Sarita around has brought the joy of those days back to me. I really love kids. "

"I know you do."

"And Porter and Sarita are very special children. I've seen such an improvement in them over the past little while."

"Thanks. I'm working at it."

"I know you are," Julian replied.

"I hate to be so persistent, but I am your sister and I care about you a lot. So what do you think? Do you want to remarry?"

"Not at this point in my life, Catherine. But maybe later," he said with a broad grin, tickled by the fact that though he was well into his golden years, physically he looked many decades younger.

"Okay, I'm not going to push the point. For now. But I've got a ton of intelligent, beautiful friends who would love to meet a man like you."

"I'll keep it in mind, little sister. Right now I have other priorities."

"So where are we going?" I asked, as Julian rolled down the window and stuck his hand into the wind, letting it sail up and down the way kids do on hot summer days.

"I was hoping we could drive up to the cottage today. I haven't been up there in years. I thought today would be the right day for me to share The Second Mastery of the Family Leader with you."

"Really?" I replied joyfully. "I was wondering when you'd reveal this one. What does it say?"

"The Second Mastery of the Family Leader is all about trust-building and opening the lines of humanity."

"Opening the lines of humanity?"

"Yes. All too often, Catherine, we restrain our humanity. We don't tell people how much we love them or all that we appreciate about them. This failure prevents us from forging the bonds of love that give rise to a great family culture. The Second Mastery of the Family Leader says *Shift from Scolding the Child to Molding the Leader*, and that's done through deepening your relationships at home."

"Okay, Julian, let's head up to the cottage. I think that's a great idea. Jon's working on a big project and said he'd be home later than usual. I could call his mom and ask her to pick Porter up from school. I know she'd be thrilled to have the kids all day."

"Excellent," replied Julian, clearly pleased at my willingness to rearrange my schedule so we could be together for a full day of learning.

"And, to be honest, I could use the break. I've been spending so much time with the children that I'd love some time off in the country."

"It's important to have your time too, Catherine. Too many parents feel guilty if they take some time for themselves. They think it is a selfish thing to do. But carving out time to renew and recharge is actually a very selfless act."

"Really?"

"Of course. It makes you better with your whole family. When you are happy, they will be happy. When you feel relaxed and at peace, you will be at your best. And your family will benefit the most."

"Excellent point. I'll remember that one."

"So let's drive straight out to the country. I want to share a few more principles with you that I know will make your home life even better. You're doing some great things these days. I'm very impressed with all your efforts. That chat we had down at the BraveLife.com offices really seems to have made an impact."

"You opened my eyes to a lot of things on that day, Julian. The whole notion that I need to be a leader at home and build a unique family culture really hit the mark."

"I'm glad," came the soft reply.

What Julian referred to as "the cottage" was really a spectacular estate property that my grandfather had built on forty-two acres of the most beautiful grounds you could ever imagine. The home overlooked a magnificent freshwater lake that we used to swim in and boat on as children. Flowers were everywhere, and the sounds of singing birds could be heard throughout the property. It was so good to be back.

As we drove along the road that led to the main house, my mind was drenched with memories of the past. I remembered the day Julian taught me how to sail the boat that our mother had bought for us the day we finished school that year. We both had placed at the very top of our classes, and she said she'd get us something special. We spent day after lazy summer day in that sailboat, making up hilarious stories and dreaming about the lives we would create as adults. Even back then, Julian's dream was the same: "I'm going to be a great trial lawyer," he would say.

I smiled as I thought about the night when, as kids, we slept outside under the stars and told tales of ghosts and goblins to each other, growing so frightened that we had to yell for our father to come out and escort us inside with the aid of a flashlight. And I recalled all the great family times we had enjoyed at this idyllic retreat, times so grand it seemed that happiness and love infused the very air we were breathing.

"I always loved the smell of these flowers in the spring," observed Julian in a relaxed tone.

"Me, too. I've never been able to find flowers this big in the city," I replied.

Walking up the path to the big house, Julian threw an arm over my shoulder and then continued along the way silently.

"You know why we both love this place so much?" he asked after a few moments.

"Tell me?"

"It's because of the memories, Catherine."

"The memories?"

"Yes. Sure, this is a marvelous place. But at the end of the day, the reason why this property has such a place in our hearts is because of all the human moments we have enjoyed here."

"Human moments?" I answered, curious about yet another of Julian's novel phrases.

"Yes, *human moments*. The *Harvard Business Review* did a piece on this subject a number of years back. The author wrote that the reason people are no longer happy, creative, and inspired at work is because the modern workplace has grown so busy there is no longer a place for human moments."

"What exactly are human moments?"

"They are those special times when human beings come together and connect in a deep, open way. Before things in the corporate world became so busy and fast-paced, we used to make time to chat at the water cooler about what we did on the weekend or ask our co-workers about the progress their children were making. We would get to know our colleagues and come to see them as important elements in the fabric of our lives. Now, people come in to work and are assaulted by a barrage of e-mails, a never-ending stream of voicemail, and a mile-high pile of faxes. In the new business world, we no longer have the time to slow down, enjoy each other's company, and connect warmly. We practically don't even know these people that we spend the better parts of our days with."

"And the thing that's ironic," I added, "is that when we find the time to foster these connections that you're speaking of, innovation, productivity, and on-the-job effectiveness soar."

"That's exactly what this consultant wrote in the article. But I think that his real point was this: business leaders can enrich the spirit of the communities of people that comprise their companies by encouraging human moments at work."

"I think I know where you're going with this one," I said intuitively.

"Apply the same thinking to your home life," stated Julian.

"Interesting."

"To show real leadership within your family," Julian continued, "encourage human moments between yourselves. Stop scolding the children and start molding and sculpting them into leaders through the gift of your unconditional love. All effective leaders care deeply about the relationships that comprise their organization. You shouldn't be any different."

"Agreed," I said in a reflective tone, knowing that work still needed to be done with that fiery temper of mine that I'd sometimes let loose during those times when the kids were screaming, phones were ringing, and deadlines were approaching quickly.

"You are a star in business, Catherine," Julian continued, making me feel a little better. "I'm certainly not in a position to lecture you on the art of growing a world-class enterprise. You've done that and have succeeded admirably."

"Thanks, Julian."

"And given your experience as a corporate leader, you know that ultimately what makes a great business is great talent. Great, creative, energized people who are passionate about what they do."

"Completely correct," I replied as we walked into the grand living room of the dwelling.

"And I know you will also agree that the best way to bring out the best in people is to show them that you truly care about them."

"I do."

"So the heart of business success lies in connecting to people's hearts. *True leadership of human beings lies in commending them rather than in condemning them.* The deeper your relationship with others, the more effective your leadership of them will be. People will not follow you if they don't trust you. And here's the big lesson," Julian spoke with heightened emotion: *"Before anyone will lend you a hand, you must first touch their hearts."*

"Before someone will lend you a hand, you must first touch their heart? I love that one, Julian."

"Know why you love that one?"

"No, why?"

"Because it speaks to the truth. Every human being, no matter what stage of evolution they are at, has the capacity to recognize the highest truths of humanity. And that phrase I just mentioned is one of them."

"Wow. It reminds me of a quote I recently read by the German poet Goethe where he wrote: 'Treat people as if they were what they ought to be and help them become what they are capable of being.'"

"And that is what human moments are all about. Those little opportunities to show your humanity to another person. Those little windows of chance to show love and compassion for another person that reveal themselves each and every day but generally go unseized because we are all so darn busy being busy."

"And seizing these opportunities to create 'human moments' deepens our relationships in profound ways, right?"

"Right. And not only that. These human moments leave us with indelible memories which, at the end of the day, are the most precious things in life. You see, Catherine, a great life is nothing more than a series of great memories woven together."

"Fascinating."

"It's true. All too often we get caught up in thinking that we need to achieve certain heroic acts in order to validate our lives and bring us great success. We get fooled into believing we must accumulate expensive toys and an excess of belongings in order to be fulfilled at the end of the day. But that's not the way to real happiness. *Real and lasting happiness comes through the progressive accumulation of lovely memories and special moments.* For the rest of your days, Catherine, commit yourself to doing whatever it takes to collect as many great family memories as possible. *And remember that the best way to be really really successful in life is to be really really kind.* Take all that thinking from the corporate environment about community building and human moments and transpose it into your home life. Bring these tried and true leadership philosophies of the business world into the four corners of the place where you live."

"How exactly?" I wondered.

"Start thinking that the deeper your relationship with Jon and the kids, the more effective your leadership will be within your home. Stop scolding Porter and Sarita and start molding them into the great souls that we both know they are destined to become."

"And stop condemning and start commending them?" I added, borrowing Julian's phrase.

"Right on," Julian replied excitedly, jumping up into the air as if he were riding a trampoline. "Praise your kids on jobs well done. *Never forget that behavior that is rewarded is behavior that gets repeated.* Recognize and appreciate them when they help with the dishes or prepare dinner with you. Lavish them with sincere praise when they learn a new skill or try a new game. *Sincere praise is one of the finest motivators of the human heart and yet we rarely use it.*"

"I guess you're right, Julian. We restrain our humanity."

"And don't be so quick to get mad when they spill a little milk or break a brand new dish. They are children and that's what children do. It's one of the ways that they learn. I remember one of the investment bankers I used to hang out with in my old glory days telling me that the secret to the incredible confidence that he had stemmed from his childhood."

"What in particular?"

"Well, he was raised by his father, and whenever he would spill a drink or break a dish or make a mistake, his father, rather than getting angry, would ask him: 'So, Jerry, what's the lesson here?' That simple question led to the forging of one of the strongest characters I've ever known. Remember, Catherine, a mistake is only a mistake if you make it twice. The first time around it's a learning experience, one essential for growth."

"Really?"

"Of course. Wouldn't you agree that the primary way we grow as people is through our failures and mistakes?"

"For sure. Come to think of it, my biggest setbacks have led to my greatest growth."

"Exactly. Failure is the highway to success. Failing is nothing more than learning how to win. *Good parents reward excellent failures.* When Porter and Sarita have the bravery to step out and try something new and they fail, reward and encourage them. It will flood them with confidence and inspire them to keep growing and stretching their capacities. If they've made a mistake, help them learn what went wrong and then move forward. And *never* use negative or critical language with them. Condemning children causes them to shrivel up inside and extinguishes the very light that makes them so special. It's a sin the way I hear parents screaming at their kids at the grocery store over the silliest of accidents. What that shows is that *the parents* have to get their acts together—not the children."

"My goodness, you've got some brilliant insights, Julian. You must have spent hours and hours reflecting on all this stuff."

"More like years and years," came the faint reply as Julian began to stroke his robe, deep in thought.

"And also think seriously about that all-important leadership principle I mentioned to you that says that 'people will not follow you if they do not trust you.' Recognize, once and for all, that *your primary duty as a parent is to become a builder of human trust.*"

"I need to become a builder of human trust?" I asked, intrigued by this phrase.

"Yes, Catherine. Trust forms the cornerstone of every great family culture. Like I said, before someone will lend you a hand, you must touch their heart. And touching someone's heart ultimately comes through generating their trust."

"So if I want Porter and Sarita to help out more around the house, say by picking up all their toys after they finish playing with them, I need to start touching their hearts more often?"

"Yes, that's precisely what I'm saying."

"So what practical things can I do at home to become a 'builder of trust,' as you put it? How can I start deepening my relationships and creating these great memories that you say are the stuff of great family lives?"

"Well, there are so many things you can do. The first and by far the most important is to *keep your promises and commit to your commitments.*"

"Ever heard the story of the master carpenter who was just about to retire?" Julian continued.

"I don't think so."

"Well, he was set to retire after a long and dedicated career building houses. But at the very beginning of his illustrious tenure with a prominent contractor, he had been required to make a very special promise."

"Which was?"

"The carpenter had to promise the contractor that every house he built would be built as if it was the most important project he had ever been given. He had to promise that every house would be built with dedication, care, and love. Getting ready to retire, the carpenter went into his boss's office to inform him that the house he had just completed would be his last. The boss said he was sorry to see him go and asked if he would be kind enough to do a final favor for him. 'Just build me one more house,' requested the employer, 'then you're free to go.' The carpenter, who respected his boss a great deal, agreed and immediately got to work on the new house. But unlike every other house he had built over the years, he did not use the full extent of his expertise with this final one and took every shortcut he knew to finish the project in record time so he could begin his life as a retired man. He cut corners, used inferior material, and hurried to get the task over with."

"He broke his early promise," I interjected, immersed in the story Julian was sharing.

"Yes, he did, Catherine," Julian continued. "Within weeks, the house was completed and the carpenter informed his boss of this fact. 'Thanks for doing this for me,' he said to the carpenter in a gentle tone. Then the employer handed the carpenter the keys to the front door. 'These are for you. The house you just built is my parting gift for all your years of hard work and dedication.' The carpenter was astounded. He could not believe that the home he had just built was his own. If he had known this, he would have put his very best into it."

"Wow. Great story."

"See, that carpenter failed to keep the most important promise he had made to his employer and to himself, the promise that he would do his work with excellence and true mastery of his craft. And because he breached this core commitment, he ended up living in the only inferior home that he had ever built. And so it is with our lives. We break promises and end up living in less than ideal circumstances, circumstances that we have created by our own actions."

"So family leaders must always keep their promises and remain true to their word," I concluded.

"Yes, unless they wish to end up living in inferior and miserable homes. And it's not just the promises they make to their family members that they must follow through on, Catherine. They must also keep the promises that they make to themselves. Keeping the promises you make to others builds family trust and enriches the home culture. Keeping the promises you make to yourself builds self-trust and enriches your personal character."

"That's definitely true, Julian. As you know, I've started working out regularly."

"I've noticed. You've never looked better."

"Thanks, big brother. Well, when I miss even one of

the workouts I've planned, I feel so bad. It's like I've let myself down or something."

"You have. Keeping the promises you make to yourself, whether the promise involves exercising or taking some time to commune with nature or even getting a massage after a hectic week, means you are being true to yourself. When you follow through on the commitments you have made to take better care of yourself, you are in effect honoring yourself. When you break these promises, you slowly lose trust in yourself. You weaken self-trust. The more promises you break, the more self-trust you lose. Eventually, you lose complete confidence in yourself as a human being. And when you've lost that, you've lost everything," stated Julian dramatically, the sunlight dancing off the shiny golden embroidery that ran along his robe.

"That makes so much sense, Julian. No one's ever taught me anything quite like this. Not in grade school. Not in high school. Not in business school. Please go on."

"Trust is the basis of every human relationship, whether at work or at home. To deepen your relationships with your family, you need to increase the trust that is there. And one of the most powerful ways to do that is to become a person of your word. Words have great power. Don't say you'll do something unless you can be sure you will do it. Try to keep every promise that you make. Try to become *meticulous with your word*. You will completely transform your life. That I can assure you."

"That sounds hard, being meticulous with my word. I mean I have so many commitments. It's not easy to follow through on all of them."

"Then stop making so many. Begin to underpromise so you can always overdeliver. Become more *selective* in what you promise. To be a great leader at home, you must first be a model of integrity. You must be the kind of person who does the right thing every time. The kind of person who lives by a private code of honor. In doing so, you will gain the respect of other people. Even more important, *people who keep their promises gain credibility.* Their family comes to rely on them and deeply believe in what they say—"

"Because they know it is the truth," I interrupted excitedly.

"Yes, because they know it is the truth. And the truth really will set you free, little sister."

"I've never thought that gaining credibility in the eyes of my family was that important. I've always thought that there were other priorities for me as a partner and parent."

"Credibility is key, Catherine. Credibility promotes trust, and trust, as I have said, lies at the heart of every deep, meaningful relationship. So my suggestion to you is: don't make a promise to someone or make a commitment unless you are certain you can deliver on it. Don't say you will take Porter and Sarita to the circus this weekend unless you are sure you can take them. The promises of parents mean the world to little kids. Understand that when you break these promises, you break their hearts. And do not tell Jon that you will help him write up that new business plan he has been talking about unless you are positive that you'll be able to do it. Within a very short period of time, you will see something wonderful start to happen in your life. The members of your family will start listening to you in a way they have never listened to you before. They will deeply respect you. They will come to know and love you as a person who is always true to her word. And that will build the love between you all."

"Amazing knowledge. And yet it's profoundly simple stuff."

"'Simply profound stuff' is how I'd choose to describe this wisdom that the monks were good enough to share with me," replied Julian, clearly tickled by his clever turn of phrase.

"Okay, Julian. I'm going to get really serious about keeping all my promises and committing to all my commitments. I'll become meticulous with my word. When I say I'll do something, I'll have the strength of character to do it. I will try hard to become a woman of my word—true to my word—and stop living my life according to what's easiest to do, concentrating instead on doing the right things. What else can I start doing to deepen human connections within our home?"

"Pardon me?"

"I said, what else can I start doing to deepen the human connections at home?" I repeated.

"What?"

"I said," beginning to yell and wondering if Julian's hearing was beginning to suffer in spite of his extraordinary physical condition, "what else can I start doing to deepen my human connections?"

"Run that one by me one more time, little sister."

"You've got to be kidding, Julian. I just asked you the same question three times. Why aren't you listening? It's starting to drive me a little crazy."

"Ah, thank you. Just the response I was hoping for," said a pleased Julian, grinning from ear to ear. "You've helped me segue nicely into my next point about relationship building within the home."

"I have?"

"You have. To really deepen your human connections and begin to consistently touch the hearts of your family so that your entire home life improves, you must become what I call an Aggressive Listener."

"But isn't your whole message that we have to take a softer, more compassionate approach to human relationships if we want to strengthen them? What's all this about being more aggressive, Julian? I'm tired of being aggressive. I'm tired of driving hard all day long and pushing people relentlessly. That's all I did when I worked downtown."

"I'm not suggesting that you go back to those old patterns of action, Catherine. That was your former self. Stop even viewing yourself in those terms. Start living out of your imagination, not your memory."

"Ooh, I like that phrase, Julian. That's a good one."

Julian pressed forward with his teaching. "Aggressive Listening isn't about being a more aggressive person. It's all about being a more committed listener. Too many people in this fast-paced age think that listening involves nothing more than waiting until the other person has finished speaking before they jump in. Becoming a masterful listener is a lost skill in these times of over-scheduled living, and yet it is an essential way to build trust with your family. It will enrich your home culture in ways you cannot begin to imagine. You see, one of the deepest of all the Human Hungers—"

"What's a Human Hunger?" I interjected.

"We all have a series of core human needs. The sages called them Human Hungers and had taken the time to define them all. So as I was saying, we all have these Human Hungers—such as the need to actualize our talents, the need for love and community, the need to feel we are growing and learning, and the need to feel that we are contributing to the lives of others as we journey along the path of life. Another of the Human Hungers is the need to be cherished and understood. We all have a deep need to be listened to and to feel that our words have been heard by those we are speaking to. When you

Listen Aggressively, you focus every ounce of your attention on the words the other party is offering to you and listen with great empathy and care. This, in turn, sends a powerful signal to the person speaking that you respect, value, and are interested in what they are saying. And that increases the trust level within the relationship."

"I guess it goes back to what you were saying about people not lending you a hand until you touch their hearts. Aggressively listening seems like an excellent way to really connect with someone's heart."

"Yes, it is, Catherine. There are few gifts on this planet as precious as the ability to listen completely to the person you are with, in a way that shows him that he is completely understood. It's one of those rare acts of humanity that we never seem to get around to practicing. And with the greater understanding that deep listening promotes, this world would be a far better place. Understanding is the building block of love. Take Porter, for example. While he's only six years old, I know for a fact that he loves it when you give him your undivided attention. That means when he is telling you about his day at school and what he did with his buddies in the schoolyard, you are there not only in body but also in mind. You are concentrating on his words completely, even though you might feel exhausted or be facing a crisis at work. And I know this can be hard at times, but the more you practice focusing on the conversation and blocking out all distractions, the better you will get at it. Listening is a skill to be mastered rather than a talent you are born with. The more you do it, the better you get at it."

"You're right. Porter's eyes light up when I ask him questions about the things he is passionate about and then simply listen to his answers in a sincere and loving way. I know it makes him feel important."

"And understood," Julian added.

"And understood," I repeated. "Anything else?"

"Just one final point of wisdom, Catherine, and I'll be quick because I know I've given you a lot to think about this morning."

"Believe me, Julian, I'm loving this knowledge. Keep it flowing."

"Okay. The final element of the Second Mastery of the Family Leader is to *become fanatically honest.*"

"Which means?"

"Which means that no matter how hard it feels to speak the truth in a given situation and how difficult it is to let your true thoughts shine through, be honest. Say what you mean to say."

"Speak my truth?" I suggested, echoing Julian's words from a previous lesson.

"Oh you're good, little sister. Exactly. Now I should also clarify that in being fanatically honest I'm not suggesting that you be so blunt that you offend and insult people. My message is different. Being fanatically honest kind of gets back to what I was telling you earlier—it's about being meticulous with your word.

Don't treat your words lightly. They are powerful. When you say anything, make certain you mean it. When you feel strongly about something in a situation with Jon, for example, express it. Dispense with all flattery and fluff and get down to the truth in all your conversations."

"What effect does becoming fanatically honest have?" I wondered.

"A very dramatic one," responded Julian. "Like the kind of effect keeping your promises and following through on your commitments has. It deepens the trust people have in you. They know that when you say something, it's truthful. You gain immense respect in their eyes and you grow in power as a human being when you speak the truth in all circumstances. People know where you stand, and there is no longer anything fake about you. All of the superficiality that decorates most of our characters is stripped away and we become naked in our humanity. And that's powerful, Catherine, really powerful. You become more than just an individual person. You rise to the level of a force of nature and you liberate this aura around you. Believe me, people can sense this strength about you."

"Did the sages have this power?"

"In extraordinary amounts," noted Julian, looking up at the sky. "That's one of the things I remember most about those loving teachers. Each and every one of them was deeply devoted to the truth, not just in their speech but within their thoughts. Makes me think of the words of that great Roman philosopher Seneca, who wrote: 'I will govern my life and thoughts as if the whole world were to see the one and read the other.'"

"I just got goosebumps from that phrase," I remarked.

"Pretty strong words, aren't they?" observed Julian. "And the sages lived by that philosophy. Really *devoted* to the truth. As a consequence, they had this almost magical influence over me. Speaking the truth and becoming fanatically honest will lead to profound improvement in your home life, Catherine."

"And in my business life, too, I'm sure."

"Very well said. In an age where people lie all the time, believing it will get them ahead, you will stand far and above the crowd as a beacon of integrity. And believe me, little sister, integrity and decency will give you a competitive edge far more powerful than any of the latest business processes would ever be able to provide."

"I guess we need to show leadership in all areas of our lives. It reminds me of what Mahatma Gandhi once said: 'One cannot do right in one department of life whilst he is occupied in doing wrong in another. Life is one indivisible whole.' With all these lessons you are giving me, I'm starting to see how all the leadership principles that executives need to use to build great businesses are equally applicable within the context of the home and vice versa. I know you've been telling me this for months, but now it's really becoming clear. And you're so right: leadership is not the sole domain of the CEO.

Practicing leadership by seeing myself as a builder of trust and a developer of people will do wonders for all my relationships, at work and at home."

"You've got it now," said Julian, walking out onto the sprawling patio that overlooked the shimmering lake. Sunlight danced off the waves, creating a dazzling effect. Julian reached into the single pocket of his robe, pulled out a pair of sunglasses, and put them on. He looked hilarious. "Cool shades, brother," I teased.

"My eyes can't stand the glare," Julian replied. "Speaking of eyes, little sister, I want to share a poem with you." Julian then reached into his pocket and pulled out an ivory-colored piece of paper that looked both delicate and ancient. Before he read the words etched on it, he spoke.

"You are the author of your children's days."

I was taken aback by Julian's statement. Although I did not fully understand it, I felt it had special meaning and was rich in wisdom. I remained silent.

"The actions you take and the habits you make as you pass through your days will influence Porter and Sarita for the rest of their lives. *Your conduct as a parent defines the days of your children.* Your behavior will have an influence on them every day, as long as they live. All eyes are on you, Catherine. Never forget that," he stated somberly as he handed me the piece of paper that had been hidden in his robe like some buried treasure. The words on the paper read as follows:

There are little eyes upon you
and they're watching night and day.
There are little ears that quickly
take in every word you say.
There are little hands all eager
to do anything you do;
And a little child who's dreaming
of the day he'll be like you.

You're the little fellow's idol;
You're the wisest of the wise.
In his little mind about you no
suspicions ever rise.
He believes in you devoutly,
holds all that you say and do;
He will say and do in your way
when he's grown up just as you.

There's a wide-eyed little fellow
who believes you're always right;
And his eyes are always opened,
and he watches day and night.
You are setting an example,
every day in all you do,
for the little child who's waiting,
to grow up to be like you.

—Anonymous

Tears streamed down my face as I finished reading the poem. I was deeply moved by what I had just read and the depth of the sentiment expressed in those words. Julian was so right when he said "words have power" and that I had to choose mine with care. At that moment, I began to feel that being a leader within my family and becoming a world-class parent was a noble thing to do. Maybe having the courage to be a great parent and a family leader was actually a *heroic* thing to do.

All those fathers and mothers who take the time to read to their children after a long day at work and a busy night doing chores are heroes in a sense. All those single parents who step up to the plate in difficult circumstances and turn adversity into opportunity by transforming their homes into places of learning, leadership, and love for the benefit of their kids must be seen as heroes of some sort. All of those people who consciously decide to give the very best that they have to give as human beings to their children, no matter how tough it is for them to do so, need to be honored, respected, and perhaps even revered.

When we were growing up, Julian had once told me that I had one fundamental choice in my life: I could curse the darkness or I could be the one to light a candle. Recently I came across a saying from the ancient thinker Plato that spoke to this very sentiment: "We can easily forgive a child who is afraid of the dark; the real tragedy of life is when adults grow afraid of the light." I realized that showing leadership in my home made me a light, perhaps for the first time in my life. It made me a noble person. It made me a bigger person. And it made me a hero. At that moment, standing in the sun-soaked patio that had seen so many wonderful times of family, it dawned on me that the act of raising my two wonderful children into decent, caring, and strong adults would be the best work I could ever hope to do. And that realization opened my heart as it had never been opened before.

I looked up to thank Julian, but he was nowhere in sight. I felt completely alone. I surveyed the living room and then the kitchen, but no Julian. I walked out onto the vast front lawn—it was still wet from the cool morning dew of a miraculous spring day—but there was no sign of my brother there either. I grew worried. I then looked out over the lake and was stunned by what I saw. There, halfway to the buoy that floated in the middle of the water, was Julian. He had left his robe on the shore and was swimming wildly, the way he used to swim as a young boy when school had just ended and we drove up to this lake for the first swim of summer. As I looked more closely, I could see a broad smile on Julian's face. And as I listened more intently, I could hear him singing something. It was the song my mother used to sing to us as children as we drifted off to sleep.

The Third Mastery of the Family Leader™

Focus Your Child on Greatness, Not Weakness

"Far away there in the sunshine are my highest aspirations. I may not reach them, but I can look up and see their beauty, believe in them and try to follow them."
—Louisa May Alcott

"The greatest danger for most of us is not that our aim is too high and we miss it but that our aim is too low and we reach it."
—Michelangelo

THE RAIN BEAT DOWN ON THE ROOF of my car as I pulled into the underground parking lot that would lead me up to the National Museum of Art and History, where Julian had asked me to meet him on this drizzly afternoon. It had been exactly two weeks since we had spent the day at the cottage, and the lessons that he had shared had already led to some remarkable break-throughs in my role as a parent—and in my conduct as a person. The human wiring that had always determined my thought processes had begun to be reconfigured as new attitudes, outlooks, and insights began to govern my days. I had become even more positive within our home and even happier with the way our lives were unfolding.

With the leadership that I was showing to the kids and the newfound love I was giving to Jon, our family life took on an almost spiritual quality that pushed it into a whole new dimension. My guess was that as the human connections deepened, personal gifts that had slumbered within us rose invisibly to the surface. As our home became a place where respect, trust, and truth were honored, each one of us grew freer to show the feelings and talents that made us special.

I had recently read about a study performed by researchers at the University of Nebraska on what makes the happiest families in the world so happy. The study revealed a number of common traits. First, the happiest families were committed to making their family life their primary priority. To use Julian's words, they recognized that "Leadership in Life Begins with Leadership at Home." Second, the members of these families were openly affectionate with each other. Again Julian had hit the nail on the head with his advice about "human moments" and the importance of compassion within the family culture. Third, researchers found that the happiest of families all shared a healthy respect for the importance of positive communication. Just as Julian had advised me, these families believed that listening and lots of honest family discussions were essential. And fourth, it was discovered that these peak-performing families spent lots of time together. As Julian had said, it's not just quality time that is important when building a richly rewarding family life. The right *quantity* has to be in place as well.

The study also found that marital happiness could play a large part in the overall happiness of the family. When the relationship between the parents was loving and built upon mutual respect, the family unit was often more loving as a whole, and each member showed greater respect for one another's needs. When the couple got along well, the family as a whole got along well.

But as I read more and more about successful families, prompted by the inspiration that Julian had given to me over his days with us, I came to realize that the makeup of contemporary families has changed greatly. I read of single fathers making splendid parents and raising fine children. I learned of dedicated single mothers who would hold down busy jobs during the day and then would come home at night to create wonderful home environments for their children in spite of the fact that their bodies ached and their feet hurt. I found that growing numbers of grandparents were, for a wide variety of reasons, becoming primary caregivers for their grandkids, and doing extraordinarily well in the process. I had the chance to reconnect with one of my business school chums, a woman who had just undergone a painful divorce and was raising her three young children alone, discovering in the process that even though her hours were full and the demands on her were many, she had never been more fulfilled in all her life.

As I dug deeper and became more aware of this organization of human beings we call the family, I realized that this time-honored institution is going through the same dramatic change being experienced by every other organization on the planet. The traditional two-parent model, with the man working outside the home and the woman working within it, is no longer the norm. The more I looked and the wider I opened my eyes, the more I began to notice stay-at-home fathers grocery shopping with their kids in the middle of the afternoon. I became more aware of other hard-driving women executives who, like me, had decided to move their offices into their homes, and fast-track fathers who had decided to take a few years off to raise their children. I saw blended families that were the envy of their neighborhoods and intergenerational families where dinnertimes saw children, their parents, and their grandparents sitting around the table, with much laughter and love in between. The big news of our day wasn't just the rise of the New Economy fueled by high-tech companies and a new business culture. We also had to take into account the rise of the New Family—with all its permutations and non-traditional configurations— that, I discovered, is rapidly reshaping our human culture.

Riding up the elevator from the parking garage to the museum, my thoughts drifted to my own parents. My father had been a gifted man whose ambition had taken him to the pinnacle of the legal world and whose big heart had made him tops in my own. My mother was a brilliant writer who loved the arts nearly as much as she loved her children. Growing up, I had always felt that Julian was her favorite, though in her final years she let me know that this had never been the case. She loved us both with equal intensity and though Julian rarely spoke of her, I knew he missed her as much as I did. Someone once told me that "as you raise your children, so you raise your generations." I had been fortunate enough to have two great parents who, I now recognized, showed great leadership at home. They gave their generation a lovely head start, I thought.

As the doors opened, I walked into the main hall of the museum. I always loved coming to this place with its breathtaking Picassos and its spellbinding statues. These days, I tried to bring Porter and Sarita here on as many weekends as I could. Jon would meet up with us after exercising at the gym—a new habit he had adopted as part of our overall plan to live richer lives and be better role models for our children. I felt that it was important to give the children a healthy appreciation of the arts and to expose them to as many of the great creations of humankind that it was in my power to introduce them to. I knew it would eventually have a positive effect.

Julian had asked me to meet him in the Michelangelo Room. I knew he had been doing a lot of reading on the life of this great artist and respected him for the commitment to excellence he showed in his craft. I entered the room, looking for a tall, strikingly handsome man in a dazzling red robe, but Julian was nowhere to be found. The only company I had was a small group of tourists being led on a tour by a tour guide. I decided to sit down on the wooden bench and take in the sights while I waited for my brother. Part of the process of simplifying my life involved breaking my lifelong habit of feeling the need to fill every waking moment with frenzied action. I had begun to get more comfortable with taking some time for myself just to take in life's basic but beautiful moments—like the way a spider's web glistened after a rainstorm or the way the stars danced in the sky on a quiet, cloudless night. Sometimes, Jon would encourage me to take an hour for myself to browse through the wonderful secondhand bookstore that was within walking distance of our home or to retreat to the public gardens that our place backed on to.

I came to love these quieter moments of life just as much as I adored the noisy, playful times with my family. Emerson said, "Without the rich heart, wealth is an ugly beggar." In all those years that I pursued and accumulated mountains of money, I had never had a rich heart. With all the inner work I was now doing, a rich heart had finally begun to beat within me.

As I glanced at the marble statues in the room, I started listening in on the tour guide's explanations. I was struck by the depth of his knowledge and his obvious passion for the masterpieces that the museum housed. I was also a little surprised at what he was wearing. While he had on the traditional guide's uniform of a white shirt and a black tie with matching trousers, an oversized baseball cap covered the better part of his head and white flaps kept most of his face out of view. I'd seen college students wearing caps like this on spring break in Florida to protect themselves from sunstroke as they consumed barrels of beer while relaxing on the beach. I thought the tour guide looked odd but no one else seemed to notice the inappropriateness of his attire. Perhaps the tourists thought he was dressed normally for a guide and planned to buy a hat like his once the tour was over.

The guide continued to speak and the tourists continued to listen dutifully. Not one of them asked a question. Then, in the middle of a sentence, the guide did something that made me laugh. He reached into his pants and pulled out a jumbo-sized hot dog that he had squeezed into his pocket. As he munched on it, he had the audacity to continue his lecture about Michelangelo's work and its impact—food flying from his mouth all the while.

Suddenly an elderly woman from the back of the group pulled out a bottle of Dijon mustard from her purse along with a spoon and walked up to the tour guide. Without even speaking to him, she began to lavishly spread mustard over the hot dog. The guide did not say a word and the crowd didn't even seem to notice. After performing this act of service, the woman returned to her place in the crowd and the guide continued his presentation, polishing off his hot dog as he went. The whole scene seemed surreal—like something out of a weird movie that you'd watch in black-and-white in the middle of the morning when the rest of the world was asleep. But I thought it would be best if I minded my own business. I prayed Julian would show up soon.

"All great sculptors envision their works of art before they even pick up their knives," the tour guide continued, mustard dripping from his lower lip. "You see, ladies and gentlemen, all things in life are created twice: first when we dream them and then when we create them."

Hey, this guy's pretty good, I thought. "No wonder the museum lets him dress the way he dresses and do the things he does."

"In your own life," he added, pulling a granola bar from the other pocket of his pants and beginning to chomp on it, "you must create a compelling vision on the picture screen of your imagination and then live out this ideal."

"Hey, wait a minute!" I said out loud, unable to contain myself. "I've heard those words before. And come to think of it, I've heard that voice before," I exclaimed, beginning to put the pieces of this weird puzzle together. "This whole scene is far too bizarre to be real. It makes me wonder if this is some kind of a prank, a childish little prank put together by a childish big brother who's been playing these kinds of practical jokes on people ever since he was a kid."

The entire room was silent. The tourists were aghast. Finally, one of them spoke. It was the mustard lady.

"I beg your pardon, madam," she asked, looking straight into my eyes, "but what the heck are you talking about?"

"This whole thing is a joke, isn't it?" I persisted. "Julian called me up here and you are all probably people he knows posing as tourists. Right? I'm on to you all. The surprise is over. Nice job, though—you had me going for a while there," I said, clapping my hands for effect and forcing a fear grin.

The room remained silent. Then the guide spoke.

"I'd better call security. We might have a little problem here, ladies and gentlemen," he remarked as he reached for a red phone that sat on the wall amid the statues.

I became nervous, starting to doubt myself. Maybe this wasn't one of Julian's famous gags after all. My goodness, I thought, what if these people really are tourists and this guide is legitimate? Beads of sweat began to congregate in the pits of my arms. My breathing started to quicken. The Michelangelo Room was beginning to feel extremely hot. Then I caught myself and had the courage to listen to the still, small voice within me that was telling me that Julian had some part to play in this odd spectacle. I *had* to be right about this one.

With confidence renewed, I marched over to the tour guide and ripped off his hat. The crowd looked horrified. I started to laugh. Sure enough, it was Julian.

"Hey, little sister, can't a man eat a hot dog in peace anymore?" he said, before beginning to howl with laughter. The "tourists" all followed, erupting into guffaws and high-fiving Julian.

"We fooled her, Mr. Mantle," yelled the mustard lady. "We really fooled her!"

Julian reached over and gave me a bear hug, squeezing me tightly as he continued to laugh. "We really had you going for a while there," he whispered in my ear.

"Ladies and gentlemen," he said t
ing a thespian of the English stage
sister, Catherine."

The crowd roared, clapping wildly, clearly ա
the show Julian had put on.

"Thanks for helping me out today, gang," Julian said
with great warmth.

"Who are all these people?" I asked my brother.

"These fine people are all actors. They belong to the
Fernbrook Society."

"You mean that troupe of actors that wins all those
major awards every year?" I wondered.

"Yes. They're pretty great, aren't they? I won a big
case for them when I was practicing law—one of the
Hollywood studios tried to steal one of their ideas and
use it in a movie. I decided to call in the favor this afternoon."

"Anytime, Mr. Mantle," the mustard lady, obviously
the group's leader, replied graciously.

As the actors streamed out of the room, they shook
Julian's hand and patted him on the back, appearing to
accord him tremendous respect. Within a few moments,
the room was empty but for Julian and I.

"I've got to hand it to you, Julian. You're still a show-
man."

"Thanks, Catherine," replied Julian with a big smile.
"We all need to let loose once in a while."

ey, what about your robe? This is the first time I've
en you without it."

"It's at the dry cleaners," Julian laughed, his face
alight with positive energy.

"Okay, so why are we here?" I asked, getting down to
business. "I know there's got to be more to this meeting
than that practical joke you just pulled on me. By the
way, you really got my heart beating on that one. You've
pulled some fast ones on me, but that's got to be one of
the best."

"Yeah, it was pretty funny, wasn't it," noted Julian,
still chuckling. "Thanks for being such a great sport.
Well, you're right Catherine, there's another lesson I
want to share with you today. It's actually the Third
Mastery of the Family Leader, and it's certainly one of
the most important."

"And the Third Mastery is?" I asked expectantly.

"The Third Mastery of the Family Leader is to *Focus
Your Child on Greatness, Not Weakness.*"

"Wow, that sounds like another good one."

"And essential for the development of your children into
leaders and effective human beings. The Third Mastery is
all about recognizing Porter's and Sarita's strengths and
concentrating on these talents so they expand and evolve.
You see, Catherine, *most people spend more time focusing on their weaknesses than developing their strengths.
And as a result of this, most people never connect with the
greatness that it is their duty to discover.*"

"Does everyone have the potential for greatness in their life?"

"Everyone," came the unequivocal reply. "As I told you earlier, we are all here on this planet for some special reason. We all have something special to give to the world, in our own unique way. Your job as a parent is to cultivate the special strengths and top talents of your children so they shine as people and make the difference they are here to make."

"You know, Julian, what you're saying makes perfect sense. I've found that in business, for example, I used to try and be a jack of all trades. I tried to be a great communicator and a brilliant administrator. I tried to be a visionary leader and an excellent comptroller. I tried to be good at everything within the company and the result was that I was a master of nothing."

"Exactly—it's almost as if you were successful in spite of yourself, Catherine. But most people are not so fortunate. Most people try to focus on doing too many things and end up being good at none. The real key is to *specialize*."

"Specialize?"

"Yes, to become an effective leader and a peak performer on the playing field of life, you cannot be a generalist, trying to be all things to all people. All of the geniuses who have graced this planet before us had one thing in common—they concentrated their lives on cultivating the gifts that made them special. Take Einstein, for example. He had the good sense to figure out that he had a remarkable aptitude for physics, and then spent the rest of his life refining that gift. He did not move into the fields of biology or chemistry. He specialized in his core competency. And because he stayed with what he did best and dedicated years and years to this mastery, a point eventually came when he achieved greatness as a human being."

"Any other examples come to mind, Julian?"

"Well, I know you used to love rock music so how about the most brilliant guitar player of all time—Jimi Hendrix. Jimi figured out that he had an extraordinary ability to play the guitar. So rather than also trying to become good at playing the drums and the trumpet, he dedicated—no, devoted—himself to mastering his gift. For the remaining years of his life, most of his waking time was spent on the development of this passion. As with Einstein, a time eventually arrived when he achived greatness."

"But haven't you been teaching me all along that a balanced approach to life is important? I mean, this kind of devotion to the development of our human gifts sounds fairly extreme to me," I said earnestly, deeply engaged by the concept Julian was sharing with me.

"Excellent point, Catherine. Your intellect continually impresses me. But if I may make a suggestion."

"Sure."

"Begin to listen to your heart more. You see, the intellect only thinks but the heart always knows."

"What does that mean?"

"Most people spend too much time thinking and not enough time feeling. Start listening to your heart more. Begin to connect with the inner wisdom it carries. When you listen to that small voice that resides deep within you, you will know the right way to live. Yes, many geniuses have lives that can be characterized as extreme. I certainly believe that we should all strive for balance and play and peace in life. But at the end of the day, we each have a destiny that has been laid out for us. For Einstein and Hendrix, their paths required deep devotion to their personal gifts. For most people, a simple dedication to the refinement of their highest talents will bring them the success they deserve. Reach deep into your heart to find out what your path requires you to do."

"I already know what I am required to do, Julian. I'm almost certain that my path, at least for the foreseeable future, calls for me to dedicate myself to being an inspirational parent to Porter and Sarita and helping them grow into adults who are wise, decent, strong and successful. My career remains important to me, but I've achieved more in the past few years than most people will achieve in a lifetime—and I feel blessed for that. Now I feel its time I make my children my consuming occupation."

"I know that is the path you must follow," replied Julian. "And I've known it for quite some time," he added mysteriously. "And that's why the Third Mastery of the

Family Leader is so important for you. You must focus Porter and Sarita on reaching for greatness in their lives rather than letting them be consumed by their weaknesses. One of your highest duties as a family leader is to lead your children to an appreciation of their core competencies—what the sages called a person's 'special strengths' and their 'true talents.' Then you must inspire them to kindle these sparks into roaring fires that will blaze brilliantly for all the world to see. "

"But expecting Porter and Sarita to be as brilliant and famous as Einstein or Jimi Hendrix or Michelangelo is placing a little too much on their shoulders, isn't it? I mean, that would almost be setting them up for failure. I don't think I'd want to put that kind of pressure on anyone."

"You're missing my point, Catherine," noted Julian lovingly. "I'm not saying that you need to raise your kids to become the best in the world at what they do and in the way they live. I'm simply saying that they must become inspired to become the best that *they* can be. You need to lead them to realize their highest personal talents and live their best lives. In doing so, you will have fulfilled your mandate as a parent."

"The sages taught you that?"

"I told you, Catherine, these people were unbelievable thinkers. And really progressive human beings, I might add. They did not believe that deep fulfillment in life came through meditating on the top of a mountain all day. While they believed, of course, that we should carve out time daily for silence and reflection, the sages of Sivana believed that true success came through liberating our human potential and actualizing our highest talents for the greater good. *They believed that the ultimate pupose of life was to manifest our highest talents in a way that added value to the world and made it a better place to be.* It makes me think of the words of Albert Schweitzer: 'At that point in your life where your talent meets the needs of the universe, that's where God wants you to be.'"

"These sages were remarkable," I muttered gently.

"They were. And so, taking their lead, I suggest that you make it a priority to help Porter and Sarita discover and then refine their special strengths so that one day, they will reach the point of personal greatness. They will be such unique and extraordinary human beings that they will stand high above the crowd."

"But aren't they too young for that right now?" I asked, always the pragmatist.

"Nope," came the swift response. "Figuring out the special strengths and true talents of your children starts from day one, really. Often it can take years before you really discover what they are truly gifted at."

"Once Jon and I discover the special strengths and true talents of the kids, I'm still not certain what the next step is," I continued.

"After you discover these attributes, you should then help the kids become *aware* of their personal gifts so they develop an understanding of what makes them special as human beings. From there, you and Jon need to move into the cultivation stage of the process where the talents of the children begin to bloom and see the light of day. Helping the kids cultivate their special strengths and truest talents might also involve sending them to seminars or encouraging them to read books so that they continually improve on those capacities. But the real key is to encourage them to focus on their unique gifts as early as possible and for as long as possible."

"So that's what lies at the heart of the Third Mastery—Focus Your Child on Greatness Not Weakness—this imperative for us as parents to kindle the highest gifts that our children possess."

"Yup," replied Julian in a relaxed tone. "And that's why I asked you to come to this room today—the Michelangelo Room. He was quite an impressive man, I've discovered."

"Don't tell me that the sages taught you all you know about Michelangelo?"

"No, I actually learned about this man's extraordinary talents on my own through reading. And one of his organizing principles as an artist was his realization that many magnificent masterpieces began as raw blocks of marble. But through daily carving and sculpting with a steady hand and a dedicated eye, through endless industry and toil, this raw material could evolve into a sight to behold, a true work of art."

"A true wonder of the world," I added.

"Right. Michelangelo once said that 'the marble not yet carved can hold the form of every thought the greatest artist has.' But the real key to his greatness, I believe," observed Julian, "was his remarkable capacity *to execute on his vision.* He was a man of action. He recognized that it is not enough to dream big dreams and to think great thoughts. *The heart of life mastery lies in doing whatever it takes to bring the dream to life.*"

"It's just like you were saying earlier—everything begins as a vision; then it falls to the dreamer to make it all happen."

"Yes, Catherine. And this same thinking needs to be applied to your role as a parent. Your children are like blocks of marble, raw in talent and rich in potential. But you must be like a great artist, sculpting, shaping, and defining them through the leadership that you show."

"So that they can then lead the lives they are destined to live."

"Correct. So that they can live their best lives."

"So what kinds of practical tools and strategies do you have in store for me today, big brother?"

"Four in particular. The sages called these *The Four Disciplines of Personal Greatness.* And simply stated, they are: envision daily, set goals weekly, walk with giants regularly and give graciously."

"They sound intriguing. Was it only the children of the sages who practiced these four disciplines?"

"No, Catherine, everyone in the community lived by these four virtues. They felt that if they did, they would be certain to keep evolving on a daily basis. Eventually they would come to know themselves."

"I'm not quite sure I follow you, Julian. Are you saying that these extraordinarily enlightened people didn't even know who they were? I'm a bit confused."

"All of life is nothing more than a quest," came the reply after a minute's silent reflection. "Enlightened people know that the whole purpose of the game is to spend your life trying to discover who you really are and what your main aim in life is to be. The whole objective is to discover and then manifest your Essential Self."

"So you're saying the purpose in life is to discover our 'special strengths' and 'true talents'?" I asked earnestly.

"That and so much more. Discovering the gifts that make you unique as a human being is only part of it. Ultimately, the game of life is an inner game, one that is played between the ears. *Deep fulfillment in life does not come from accumulating objects but from actualizing our selves.* Life isn't about collecting nice objects, although there's nothing wrong with having them. But material pursuits shouldn't be the main purpose that drives your days. If it is, if you sacrifice time with your family and time developing yourself for time spent chasing objects, one day you will end up in a very sad state.

See, Catherine, through my own struggles and setbacks in life, I've come to the realization that *happiness in life does not come from getting, it comes from being.*"

"Can you elaborate on that a little more, please? Actually, I've been thinking about this issue almost daily. I'd love for you to shed some more light on it for me."

"Sure. What I'm saying is that the real joy of life lies in peeling back the layers of the onion."

"What? I asked you to shed some light on the subject, not to plunge me further into darkness," I replied with a grin.

"Human beings are like onions. In the center rests our highest selves, the people that we truly are. Our primary duty as people is to do all the inner work required—to peel back all the layers—until we discover our Essential Selves—our best selves. Having the right cars, houses and clothes is completely meaningless if you haven't yet caught a glimpse of the person who you meant to be. *So stop trying to get more in life and try to be more for life. That's where lasting happiness lies.*"

"But I thought you said that the ultimate purpose in life is to give—to make a difference in the lives of others through the value that we add?"

"Splendid point. You really have been doing lots of deep thinking. I'm so pleased that my time with you is time well spent. Yes, Catherine, the ultimate purpose of life is to make this world a better place through the lives we touch. *The purpose of life really is a life of purpose.*

But in order to be in a position to add real value to other people and contribute to the world as best as you can, you must first come to know who you really are as a human being. Most people have no sense of their Essential Selves or of the fundamental makeup of their characters. They've never made the time to get deep into the DNA of their lives and figure out what drives them. Most of us plod through life responding to whatever the currents of the day blow our way. We never really get into the game. But wise people—true leaders—are very different in the way they conduct themselves. They make time for themselves and the activities that involve their inner work. And by doing this, they come to know themselves."

"All of the philosophers have said this, haven't they?" I chimed in. "All their statements like 'know thyself' and 'the unexamined life is not worth living.'"

"Exactly. All of the planet's greatest thinkers have realized that we must do inner work to figure out who we really are. Only then can we create magnificent lives. Here, follow me. There's something else I want to show you in the museum."

Julian then grabbed my hand and hurried me into an adjacent exhibit hall. A sign at its entrance read "The T.S. Eliot Collection."

"This room contains many of T.S. Eliot's most famous works. I was in here early this morning and read a quote on one of these open pages. It's in his own handwriting!

Here, read it," Julian said excitedly, pointing to a yellowed page in an old book that was encased in glass for protection. The quotation read:

We must not cease from exploration. And the end of all our exploring will be to arrive where we began and to know the place for the first time.

I marveled at the power of those words. Finally, I got what Julian was saying. I mean finally, I *really* got it. We are born into perfection. Everything we need to live glorious lives is not on the outside. It's on the inside. What Julian was trying to tell me was that anyone who spends their life chasing material things in the pursuit of success is sorely misguided. Happiness does not lie at the end of that road, misery does. What my brother was telling me, in his own inimitable way, was that *the way to an extraordinary life lies in exploring ourselves, in learning of our greatest capacities and in understanding who we fundamentally are as people. Then, equipped with this essential knowledge, we can go out into the world to do what we have been wired to do and create the goodness that we have been placed here to create.* At that moment, a switch within me was turned on. Something deep inside of me had finally clicked. I realized that for my life to change in a fundamental way, *I* had to change in a fundamental way. I vowed, from the deepest recess of my heart, that I would never again sacrifice hours of my life *getting* the objects I wanted. I promised myself that from that day onwards, the focus of my life would be *becoming* the person I knew I could be.

"So back to *The Four Disciplines of Personal Greatness*," Julian said with his usual enthusiasm.

"That will help the kids live their best lives," I interjected.

"Believe me, Catherine, these four ideas will help *you* too. But yes, teaching them to Porter and Sarita will cause profound shifts in the way they conduct themselves and help them develop into the kind of adults we all dream of our children becoming. And speaking of dreaming, I'll segue elegantly into the first discipline—Envision Daily—which is all about using our creative imagination to manifest our thoughts into reality."

"Sounds kind of esoteric for me, Julian."

"Actually, like so much of the philosophy I've shared with you, it's immensely practical. The discipline of daily envisioning is all about the power of visualization and how we can improve the way we do things by creating mental templates of the way we wish to be on the drawing boards of our imaginations. I suggest that when you have a little time, you read a book called *Peak Performance* by Charles Garfield, Ph.D., which details how Olympic athletes apply the process of visualization to gain competitive advantages they would never have previously enjoyed. Through regular use of this technique, they're able to tap hidden reserves of potential and perform at the highest level in their chosen sport. I cannot think of even one elite athlete who does not know of and use visualization as part of their training process. By seeing their ideal result in their mind's eye and rehearsing this successful outcome over and over, the internal wiring of their brains becomes predisposed to manifesting that success during the competition."

"Amazing."

"It truly is. Now here's my point: if every elite athlete uses the technique of creative envisioning to help them perform at their peak, why shouldn't we share this powerful technique with our children so they too can live at the level of their potential?"

"Agreed. So how can I teach this to Porter and Sarita—or are they too young right now?"

"I know of three-year-olds who have been effectively trained in the art of visualization. Hey, let's not forget who the best dreamers on the planet are."

"Young kids?"

"Absolutely. Watch three- or four-year-olds at play. They pretend they are scaling Mount Everest or walking on the moon. They live out of their imaginations and place no limits on what they can do or be. Teaching young children visualization involves nothing more than giving them a more formal structure for the dreaming that they are already doing."

"That makes complete sense to me."

"I knew it would. And never forget what Aristotle once observed: 'The Soul never thinks without a mental picture.'"

"Fascinating."

"So here's what I suggest you do, Catherine. Every week or two, take the kids out to that great park in the neighborhood and sit underneath one of those huge oak trees. Ask them to close their eyes and breath deeply. This will help them still their minds and grow more relaxed so that the images they generate can take root more deeply."

"Okay, then what do I do?"

"Well, next begin to imagine yourselves living with the new capacity or ability you hope to have. I'll give you an example."

"Great. I think I need one."

"Let's say that you want the kids to have more courage—to be fearless. Once they are in a relaxed state sitting under that tree, ask them to imagine themselves acting in a brave way. Maybe encourage them to envision themselves climbing a tall mountain. Perhaps you could suggest that they picture a scene that has them standing up to the class bully. Whatever it is, the main thing is to encourage them to start flexing their imaginations and rewiring their brains so that the fears that are holding them back come to be replaced by the strengths that will push them forward."

"Could I use the process of creative envisioning to help Porter excel at his piano lessons?"

"Of course," replied Julian, putting his arm around me as we walked into the main hall of the museum. "In his relaxed state, tell him to imagine himself seated at the piano in the living room. Get him to really believe the scene is taking place. The more vivid the picture he creates, the more powerful the results that will follow. It's also essential that he bring his emotions into the picture. *What gets emotionalized gets realized.* Emotions drive actions. He should really *feel* that he is playing the piano and performing at the highest level he is capable of. Get him to experience what it would be like to play those lovely pieces he has been working on flawlessly. Encourage him to feel how he would feel when you, Jon and Sarita clap wildly for him as he completes his playing at a whole new level. Allow him to connect with the happiness he will enjoy as his teacher praises and congratulates him on the remarkable abilities he is displaying."

"How long should this visualization go on for, Julian?"

"Good question. For adults, I would almost say the longer the better. But with the kind of busy lives most people live, a twenty-minute session of visualization is fine. For children, even five minutes can be helpful. I guess the main point is to give them this tool. Let them know that there is a way that they can eliminate their weaknesses, improve their behaviors, conquer their fears and grow into peak performers. Let them know that as they grow, there exists this tool that will help them deal with difficulties, create a positive in the face of a negative and experience joy where others are feeling pain. It will then fall on their shoulders, as they mature, to master this technique and make it a part of the way they live."

"Okay. I think I'll go on the Internet later tonight and download a few more articles on visualization. I really want to learn more about the process and share all its benefits with the kids. It will be one of my goals for this month."

"Ah, again a perfect entry point to the next discipline," laughed Julian. "The universe really takes care of things in such a splendid way."

"Really?"

"Sure. The Second Discipline of Personal Greatness is to set goals weekly. Goal setting is such an important discipline to foster within your children, Catherine. Having clearly defined goals offers so many benefits. First, setting goals restores a sense of focus in our lives, lives that have become complicated by too many options. In this age we live in, there are simply far too many things to do at any given time. There are many distractions competing for our attention. Goals clarify our desires and help us to focus on only those activities that will lead us to where we want to go. I am reminded of the words of those extraordinary jugglers known as the Flying Karamazov

Brothers who said: 'It doesn't matter how you get there when you don't know where you're going.'"

"That's a good one," I observed with a smile.

"Setting clearly defined goals provides you with a framework for wiser choices. If you know exactly where you are going, it becomes far easier to select those activities that will get you there. The alternative is to let life act on you and give you an existence that you just don't want. 'If you don't get what you like,' noted George Bernard Shaw, 'then you'll be forced to like what you get.' Writing down your goals clarifies your intentions and, as you know so well from all your success with BraveLife.com, the first step to realizing your vision is defining it. Essentially, setting goals means that your days will be governed by your life's mission rather than by your moods."

"Nicely said, Julian," I offered encouragingly.

"Another reason goal setting is so important is that it keeps you alert to new opportunities. The discipline of setting and then reviewing your personal, professional, social, and spiritual goals every week—Sunday night works best—almost magnetizes your mind to seek out opportunities for their fulfillment. I've also found that by setting goals, I become committed to a very specific course of action. It becomes much easier to connect with the inner fire that burns within us and to engage the wellspring of motivation that exists within all of us. When I set goals, my life becomes filled with the promise of a richer existence. No matter how bad a person's life has become at a certain moment and no matter how sad and disillusioned they might feel right now, they can lift their spirits up and feel so much better through the simple act of taking out a piece of paper and writing down their dreams upon it. I guess I feel that setting worthy goals is all about kindling the slumbering passion within us."

"Really?"

"Really. Setting big, juicy goals awakens the passion within us, passion that most of us have stifled as we have grown older and more cynical about the world. Goal setting reconnects us to the sense of limitless possibility that we knew as children, and it reminds us that we really can have almost anything we want in life if our commitment to our aims runs deep enough. As Sheila Graham said: 'You can have anything you want if you want it desperately enough. You must want it with an exuberance that erupts through the skin and joins the energy that created the world.'"

"That's a lovely quote. I'd love to connect with the energy that created this world, Julian."

"Trust me, little sister, that's exactly what you are now in the process of doing," replied Julian in a mystical way.

"Oh, another key point about goal setting is to ensure that you *never leave the site of a goal without taking some action towards its advancement.*"

"Excellent point," I offered with appreciation. "That's one of the rules we have at BraveLife.com. If anyone comes up with a new idea or an important innovation, they must do something to put the idea into play. It's not enough to just come up with it. The employee must act on it. That might mean making a phone call to explore the new idea's viability. It might mean writing up a one-page proposal and submitting it to me. It might mean making a presentation to the rest of the team. But the key is to get the idea into play. To get some momentum behind it. Otherwise, we all know that life will get in the way and the idea will die a quick death."

"I agree completely, Catherine. Each and every person on the planet comes up with ideas that have the potential to revolutionize our lives. Some choose to act on them and in doing so create great lives. Others choose to sit on them—and resign themselves to the ordinary."

"You make goal setting sound like such a magical process, Julian."

"Well, as a Harvard-trained lawyer, I'm always reluctant to use the term 'magic.' But I have learned through my own experience that goal setting works wonders. It makes no sense not to become excellent at this process and to teach it to your children. Sure, they might be too young right now to have concrete professional goals and the like. But the key is to expose them to the process and let them see for themselves how well it works. It's all part of your duty as a parent to let the 'bigness' of your children shine through."

"The bigness of my children?" I asked, struck by the power of this new phrase.

"Sure, another one of your primary duties as a parent is to make sure that your kids don't fall into the trap nearly every adult on earth falls into."

"Which is?" I inquired, my attention completely captured.

"Most of us live small lives. We think small. We act small and we play small."

"Adults play small?"

"We do. We don't step out onto the skinny branch of life and take bold risks. We think the same thoughts, do the same things and act the same way every day. We live our lives in an illusory zone of security, believing it is the safest place to be."

"When it's actually the *least* secure place to be," I chimed in, proud of the lessons I had learned through my time with my brother.

"Exactly. Life is truly lived when you enter the zone of the unknown. We are fully alive only in those moments when we are stretching ourselves beyond our normal limits and reaching for the stars—in some way or another. Playing small is the road to a mediocre life. Letting our bigness shine through is the path to mastery."

"And risks are a way to live a bigger life?"

"Yes, Catherine, so long as they are wise, calculated risks. No one is suggesting that you teach your children to do foolish things. My point of wisdom is that you can lead them to an understanding of the fact that they need to be willing to dare more often. They must listen to the call of their hearts regularly. If they get a big idea that will help them improve one of the core areas of their lives, they must have the courage to act on it. Remember, being a great leader in life is all about taking action."

"So teach them to take smart risks and dare more often. Right?"

"Yes, and back to the Second Discipline of Personal Greatness—make sure they develop the ritual of setting goals on a weekly basis, even if it's just a goal or two relating to what they want to see manifested in their lives over the coming week. One very specific suggestion I have for you and the kids is that you work with them to create a Dream Book."

"What's a Dream Book?" I asked.

"It's an empty writing pad that each of you can keep to fill with your goals. Think of it as a vessel within which you and the kids can capture your desires. You can list each and every one of your goals and dreams in it and record your highest aspirations. You can paste pictures of your heroes, the things you want and the places you wish to visit within it. You can jot down great quotes and inspirational words throughout it. It's an excellent way to get your kids into goal setting and, more importantly, goal getting."

"I love the idea, Julian! A truly splendid idea. I feel motivated already."

"Here, little sister," said Julian, grabbing my hand and leading me into a tiny room that I had never noticed before. The title "Gallery of the Greats" was marked over the entrance in bronze lettering.

"I've never been in here before," I remarked as we passed a series of breathtakingly beautiful and lifelike portraits of many of history's greatest women and men.

"It's brand new, actually. I just discovered this room myself. I can spend hours in here, just feeling the energy of these great human beings and reflecting on the way they conducted their lives. I always leave feeling inspired and committed to the path that I am on."

"Does coming in here have something to do with the Third Discipline of Personal Greatness?"

"You bet it does," replied Julian as he did a quick twirl and punched his fists into the air. "Oooh, I love this discipline!" he shouted.

"Okay, okay—let's hear it."

"The Third Discipline of Personal Greatness, a discipline I know will have a wonderful impact on Porter and Sarita's lives, is to 'walk with the giants regularly.'"

"Now you know I need some clarification on that one," I remarked, fascinated, as I crossed my arms and sat down on the single bench in the center of the room.

"'Walking with the Giants' is all about spending time with history's greatest people. Letting the most remarkable people of this world become your mentors of the mind. Would you like to spend some time with Mother Teresa later tonight?" asked Julian with a twinkle in his eye.

"You bet."

"How about relaxing with Nelson Mandela or reflecting with Gandhi?"

"Count me in," I offered, not quite sure where Julian was going with this line of questioning.

"You see, the gift of the knowledge age we live in is that you and I, and everyone around us, have the privilege to spend time, each and every day if we so choose, with the greatest thinkers who have walked on earth. With nothing more than a library card, you can expose your children to the innermost thoughts of Mahatma Gandhi. With nothing more than an Internet connection, you can get deep into the mind of Helen Keller or Ben Franklin or Confucius or Albert Schweitzer. You can find out what made these leaders laugh and cry. You can discover how they handled adversity. You can learn the organizing principles by which they lived out their lives. To me that's amazing. We can befriend the world's most amazing people—whenever we want—through books, tapes, videos and other educational media. And here's the real key, Catherine: in spending time with history's wisest human beings, you cannot help but come away from the experience a fundamentally better person. It makes me think of the words of author Dorothea Brande who remarked: 'I found the idea which set me free. I was not consciously looking for it. I was engaged on a piece of research in a different field. But I came across a sentence in a book I was reading which was so illuminating that I put the book aside to consider all of the ideas suggested by that [one sentence]. When I picked the book up again, I was a different person.' Associating with great minds is definitely one of the best ways to improve the quality of your own mind. It's like when you play someone who's better than you in tennis."

"You always play better than you've ever played," I replied, having experienced this phenomenon on more occassions than I cared to recall.

"Right. So when you read the books of our world's mental, philosophical, scientific, and spiritual giants on a regular basis, the way you think and act will improve correspondingly. You will rise to their level. You will find yourself thinking thoughts you have never thought before and behaving in positive ways that just might startle you. So carve out some time every week or so to expose Porter and Sarita to the works and the thoughts of the giants among us—men and women who have made major contributions to our civilization. Introduce them to the geniuses of our past as well as the leaders of our future. When you are driving them to soccer practice or ballet lessons, play compact discs of the biographies of Einstein or Mozart or

Thomas Edison. You can be certain that their influence will play a significant role in the shaping of the characters, inspiring your two wonderful children to be more than they could otherwise have been. As Thomas Bailey Aldrich wrote: 'A person is known by the company their mind keeps.'"

"And Gandhi once said, 'I will not let anyone walk through my mind with their dirty feet,'" I added, having recently read the autobiography of this great leader.

"Lovely, Catherine. He clearly understood that what you put into your mind affects the way your life will unfold."

Julian continued. "I find my companions in the 'books of the giants' that I read. You see, little sister, to me great books represent hope. They represent the promise of a better life. They help me envision a wiser and better world. And that makes books, and the daily habit of reading them, one of life's most important pursuits."

"Since Porter and Sarita are still so young, maybe I can begin to collect these great books you speak of. I still have to travel a little bit for my work with BraveLife.com and often have a few hours to kill at the airport. They always seem to have excellent bookshops."

"Of course," responded Julian. "Very successful people often fly. And very successful people always read. Booksellers have figured that out and put their best selections in those bookstores."

"I could visit some of those great shops and find some amazing books that can inspire and influence the kids as they continue to grow."

"That's a wonderful idea, Catherine," replied Julian. "In those stacks of books you will find gems of wisdom about raising children who are strong of mind, body and character. You will discover books that will help you balance career and family. You will see books that will inspire you to be your best self and books that will illuminate the path that you are destined to follow. For every possible question that you may have, you will find a book overflowing with answers. All it takes is the initiative to find the right books and then the discipline to read them."

"Say, Julian, speaking of discipline, what are your thoughts on disciplining children? That's always been a challenge for me in my home life, even though I have never had any problem disciplining employees at BraveLife.com. I find that when it comes to my kids, I find it hard to say no."

"The essence of parenting well, when it comes to discipline, is to always follow the high road rather than the easy road. Always do what your heart and conscience tell you is the right thing to do, based on your morals and on your values, rather than what you might feel is the easy thing to do in that given moment."

"It goes back to that point you made earlier. Leadership is all about doing what's right."

"Yup. And you also need to remember that discipline is a gift."

"What do you mean by that?"

"Many parents believe that constantly giving in to the demands of their children and never saying no shows their children how much they love them. But what they forget is that children need clear boundaries. They crave consistent standards that give their lives structure. Though they may not tell you this, when parents enforce limits and ensure that family rules are followed, these limits make children feel loved. Employing a reasonable amount of discipline also builds character within your kids, since they are given a true sense of what is right and wrong in every given circumstance."

"That's so true, Julian. Even though I never liked the way Mom and Dad kept us in line, secretly I knew it was a sign of their love for us. I think I've been letting Porter and Sarita get away with too much for too long. I think I must be a little stricter with them."

"Just don't overdo it, Catherine. It's all about balancing the importance of discipline with the importance of letting children be children. And also remember, when it comes to any form of punishment, always correct the behavior rather than the child."

"Elaborate, please."

"It's so important not to damage children's self-esteem. When they do something wrong, make sure that you tell them that it was *their behavior* that was bad—not them. It is so important for you to give them unconditional love and let them know that you adore them no matter what they do. Having said this, there are certain rules and limits that need to be enforced. Your children should know that whenever they step outside of these limits, they will be disciplined."

"That makes sense, Julian. It is true that the self-esteem of children is fragile. Words that they hear when they are young stay with them for many years into their futures."

"Quite true. I'd also suggest that you never discipline your children when you are angry."

"Really?" I wondered, genuinely surprised at this kernel of advice.

"Yes, the whole purpose of discipline is to help a child channel her energies in more appropriate ways. It should never serve as an outlet for a parent's frustrations. Never use it as a tool for the release of your stress, a way to make you feel better when you are angry at your child for some misdeed. Save it—and honor it—as a tool for the character development of the kids. Only then will it have the effect you hope it will."

"And the final discipline, the Fourth Discipline of Personal Greatness, is the discipline of giving graciously. This is all about the importance of teaching your children the gift that is giving with an open hand and an open heart. Remember that *the hand the gives is the hand that gathers and that giving begins the receiving process.* He or she that gives the most wins. This is one of the timeless laws of humanity that we forget all too often. Teach

Porter and Sarita the importance of remaining focused on helping others and appreciating people for the value they add to the world. Make it a practice to give the gift of praise to someone who deserves it on a regular basis. When you visit one of your friend's houses with the children, always bring a gift so the kids pick up on this habit. It does not have to be elaborate. It is the thought that truly counts. It could be something as simple as the gift of a fresh flower from your backyard or a card that the children have made out of construction paper. It could be the gift of a warm hug or a big smile. Soon they too will get into the discipline of giving and will realize how great it feels to share with others. They will connect to a higher part of themselves and experience great growth in the process. Once they discover how powerful it is to be kind and giving on a daily basis, they will have learned one of life's most significant lessons."

"Thanks, big brother," I replied with heartfelt conviction. "I love you."

"I love you too, Catherine. Oh, before I forget, I have a gift of my own for you."

Julian reached into the pocket of the pants he was wearing and pulled out a rumpled napkin that bore traces of mustard.

"I know it doesn't look like much, but the words I have written on this napkin are worth their weight in gold. I suggest you have them printed on a plaque that you can put up in a place at home where everyone can read it. Do you mind if I read them to you?" requested Julian, growing emotional, tears filling his eyes.

"Please go ahead," I said with gentleness.

"I don't know why these words resonate with me as strongly as they do. I connect so deeply to them, and they offer me such guidance. I guess they capture the essence of the life I dream of living and speak to the person I hope to be."

Julian read the words, a quote of Willian Penn:

I expect to pass through life but once. If therefore, there be any kindness I can show, or any good thing I can do to any fellow being, let me do it now, and not defer or neglect it, as I shall not pass this way again.

As Julian and I strolled out of the museum arm-in-arm it started to rain ever so slightly.

"In India, it is believed that a light sprinkling of rain is an omen of good things to come," said Julian in a voice so soft I could barely hear it. He then looked up at the sky as the raindrops danced off his face. With his eyes closed and a titanic-sized smile on his face, Julian paused for a few moments and then yelled out in a voice so loud it stopped people in their tracks: "It's a great time to be alive!"

With a mind filled with rich leadership lessons and a heart more open than ever before, I could not help but agree.

The Fourth Mastery
of the Family Leader™

To Be an Excellent Parent, Become an Excellent Person

*"Life's like a play: it's not the length
but the excellence of the acting that matters."*
—Seneca

*"The only devils in the world are those running
in our own hearts. That is where the battle
should be fought."*
—Mahatma Gandhi

IT WAS A VERY STRANGE message. Miss Williamson, my reclusive neighbor—the one who lived with fourteen cats and the one who I had jokingly suggested had a crush on Julian—had left me a voicemail message requesting that I turn up in the garden she tended behind her house. Even more odd was the fact that she asked that I be there at

5 A.M. the following morning. "Trust me, Catherine," she muttered in her squeaky voice, "there's a gift waiting for you right by the tomato patch."

Now I have to tell you that calling Miss Williamson an eccentric does not do the woman any justice. She was one of the most unique people I had ever met, and I could never understand why she lived as she did. But she was a loyal neighbor and she always offered me a smile when I passed her in the neighborhood, so I called her back and told her that I'd be happy to show up in the garden at the desired time.

Early the next morning, after showering and softly kissing Jon and the kids, I crept out the side door and walked down the street. As I made my way across Miss Williamson's front lawn, three cats jumped out from behind a shrub and scared the living daylights out of me. I just stood there for a few seconds, startled, my heart beating madly, out of control. Quickly pulling myself back together, I carefully walked around the house to the backyard and then into the large garden that she devoted many of her waking hours to. I couldn't believe what I saw.

Right next to the tomato patch was a towering scarecrow that appeared to be over six feet high. It was covered with a frilly cloth that I guessed Miss Williamson had bought at a garage sale, and was standing in one of those bizarre yoga postures I'd observed yogis taking up in documentaries Jon, the kids, and I had watched on the

Discovery Channel. Equally inexplicable was the large banner that ran from the scarecrow's body to Miss Williamson's back porch. On it was inscribed a quote by Mark Twain, written in bright red lettering that seemed to leap off the plastic background in the golden rays of the early morning sun. The quote read simply:

If everybody was satisfied with himself, there would be no heroes.

And breaking the stillness of the dawn was music, loud music that was playing from a boombox that someone had strategically placed on the picnic table nearby. The song was unmistakable. It was the great Louis Armstong's "What a Wonderful World." I just stood there, basking in the positive energy of this extraordinary sight. I had no idea what was going on. I had no idea why I had been summoned here. And to be completely honest with you, I didn't really care. Something miraculous had been growing in my life since Julian had returned, and I was just so happy to be perceiving this, day by day. This was just another experience that I knew would make a brilliant story for my grandkids.

"Miss Williamson? Are you here?" I yelled, trying to make my voice heard above Louis's crooning.

When I received no response, I tried again.

"Hello! Miss Williamson, are you out here?"

Again, no reply. Just Louis completing the song with the words "I said to myself . . . what a wonderfuuuuul wooorld."

Finally the garden was silent, and I made my way toward the tomato patch and the hilariously attired scarecrow. All of a sudden, a booming, deep voice sang out, "I say to myself, this is a wonderful world." I looked around but I could see no one around me. As I continued along the garden path I heard the voice again. "Wonderful world!" was all that rang out this time around. The sound seemed to be coming from the vicinity of the scarecrow, right next to the tomato patch. "Maybe this has something to do with the gift Miss Williamson promised me in her voicemail," I thought.

As I drew nearer, the word *wonderful* appeared to emanate from the scarecrow's lips, lips that were nearly masked by the billowy black cloth that covered the rest of its face and circled its head. This charade had Julian's name written all over it, but I knew he wasn't here because he was vacationing in Connecticut, where he had signed up for a seven-day personal growth retreat.

"I need to get even deeper into myself," he remarked as we dropped him off at the airport.

Just as I reached the scarecrow, the words "If everybody was satisfied with himself, there would be no heroes" belted out of the boombox. I felt a little scared. Who was behind this setup and why would they involve me in it?

Suddenly the scarecrow started to move. Slowly at

first—then it started to wave its arms and legs in a frenzy. Soon it was twirling round and round in the tomato patch looking like a whirling dervish. After falling to the ground in dizziness, the scarecrow came to rest. Then it started to laugh. And laugh. And laugh.

Clearly there was a man under the disguise, and clearly it was a man that I knew. I reached down and pulled the cloth off the scarecrow's face. Sure enough, the Prince of Pranks had struck again. It was Julian.

"I thought you were in Connecticut reconnecting with your highest self?" I said in mock anger, quite aware that a smile was growing on my face. "Don't you have anything better to do with your time than to set up these scenarios and scare the heck out of me?"

"I quite enjoy these pranks, little sista," replied Julian. "Things get kinda lonely from time to time when you wake up with the sun every morning."

"Well now, why don't you tell me what this lesson is all about. I can't believe you recruited poor Miss Williamson for this practical joke. She's almost ninety years old, you know."

"She loved the idea and thinks I'm hilarious," responded Julian as he looked up to the balcony of Miss Williamson's second-floor bedroom.

"Hi, Julian," she bellowed, leaning on the railing in her housecoat in between laughs. "Boy, you are good. That was one of the funniest things I've seen in a long time. C'mon in for a cup of tea after you're finished with

Catherine. I'd love to hear more about your adventures in India. Ta ta, handsome," she concluded in a sensual voice I'd never heard before.

Julian just winked at me.

"Still the charmer," I noted.

"Hey, she's a lovely woman and besides, she brews the best chamomile tea I've ever tasted."

"But seriously," I said, "I thought you were at your spiritual retreat. How come you're back?"

"I know it's not the most responsible thing I've ever done, Catherine, and I apologize for that, but my intuition told me that I had to share the Fourth Mastery of the Family Leader with you sooner rather than later. Since my time with the sages up in Sivana, I've grown far more aware of what they referred to as the 'silent whisperings from within.'"

"Oh, spare me all this mumbo-jumbo, Julian," I responded, surprised at my impatience, which I attributed to the ungodly hour.

"I'm completely serious. We all have a hidden ability to detect the truth in all circumstances in our lives. When we do all the inner work necessary to connect with our highest selves, this power—what most people know as intuition—becomes very obvious. My intuition told me that you needed to hear what I have to tell you about the Fourth Mastery far more than I needed a week of reflection and personal development. And so I'm here, at your service," Julian joked as he bent down and mimicked a butler bowing to his boss.

"And do tell me what all this stuff about 'If everybody was satisfied with himself, there would be no heroes' has to do with me."

"It has everything to do with you, Catherine. The fact that we are here in a garden has everything to do with you. The fact that I arranged for Mr. Armstrong's famous song to be played has everything to do with you."

"Get to the point, big brother," I prodded.

"The Fourth Mastery of the Family Leader is about becoming the person you were meant to be. It's about becoming your best self and realizing the full potential of your mind, body, and spirit so you can be a great leader in your family. It's about becoming a hero in your life," noted Julian with a gentle look.

"What is the Fourth Mastery of the Family Leader, Julian?" I asked good-naturedly, my mood improving as my interest in this next life lesson grew.

"It can be stated simply—like all great principles of effective living. *To Be an Excellent Parent, You Must Become an Excellent Person.* This mastery is all about self-renewal and self-regeneration."

"I'm not really familiar with that last term you used."

"What would you think of a corporation that spent no money or time on research and development?" came his precise reply.

"Not much. I certainly would never invest in it," I said.

"Right. Neither would I."

"Oh, don't tell me you're playing the stock market again, Julian. I can just see the headlines now: 'Millionaire lawyer turns enlightened monk and makes a killing in the market. With his riches, he buys a Ferrari,'" I giggled.

"My days of investing in the market are over. But my days of investing in myself have just begun. And it's the best investment I've ever made. See, you would not sink a penny into a company that paid no attention to improving on a daily basis, and yet most people in the world we live in fail to spend even one hour a month developing themselves. That's why I love the saying, 'If everybody was satisfied with himself, there would be no heroes' so much. *The people who really get on in this world and live big lives—personally, professionally, or spiritually—are those who are never satisfied with themselves. They are constantly pushing the envelope of their potential and growing stronger, wiser and more effective.*"

"But isn't there something to be said for being satisfied with yourself and liking the person that you are?"

"I'm not saying that you should not love who you are and be grateful for all your personal gifts. I'm simply saying that we should not fall into the trap of being complacent. More important, I am saying that we need to continually strive to make our lives wonderful. Wonder-full," Julian emphasized.

"Ah," I sighed, "now I get why you played that music and sang that song."

"Now you're cookin'," Julian replied, kissing me on the cheek.

"I still don't know why we are here in the garden, though."

"The garden is a perfect metaphor for the idea of self-renewal and personal regeneration. It's the ideal example of how nature rewards care, cultivation, and attention. Miss Williamson spends most of her days in here, tending to these vegetables, ensuring that they are properly cared for and given the best environment in which to grow. And 'as she sows, so does she reap.' She puts a great deal of time in and nature inevitably yields a rich harvest. It's the same for people. Taking time out of your busy schedule every day for a little self-renewal and personal regeneration will yield positive results in every area of your life."

"What exactly do you mean by self-renewal, Julian? Are you talking about making time to exercise and eat well?"

"That and so very much more." Julian paused and then led me to the picnic table. As he poured me a glass of fresh tomato juice, he continued his discourse on the Fourth Mastery.

"Remember when you were on that ill-fated flight?"

"Sad to say I do," I responded softly.

"Think about the instructions of the flight attendants."

"Well, they told us to remain calm. Not to panic. To put our heads on our legs."

"What did they say about the oxygen masks?"

"Well, every time I'm on a plane, the flight attendants tell us to do the same thing."

"Which is?"

"Essentially, they tell us to make sure we get the oxygen masks up to our own faces first before we try and help other people with their masks."

"Perfect answer," noted Julian, happy with my reply. "That's exactly what the Fourth Mastery of the Family Leader and the concept of self-renewal is all about."

"I'm still a little lost," I confessed as I began to sip the juice.

"Before you can help others, you must help yourself. To be a better parent, you must first become a better person. To manage your family in an excellent way, you must first manage yourself in an excellent way. What I'm really saying is that leadership on the outside begins with leadership on the inside."

"I'd agree with that," I observed.

"You can't do great things for your kids unless you first think great thoughts," continued Julian, clearly energized and rolling along like a Baptist preacher.

"True," I sang out.

"You can't do good in your life unless you feel good."

"True again," I said with a nod.

"And you cannot really love your children unless you first love yourself," Julian wailed.

I fell completely silent. That last statement hit me hard. Then it moved me to tears. Julian's wisdom pierced my soul. He was *so* correct. How could I really give love to the children and to Jon if I had not discovered self-love? How could a human being really show love to another unless she first found love for herself? What my brother was telling me was that before I could ever hope to become the kind of parent Porter and Sarita deserved, I needed to get serious about developing myself and "leading from the inside out."

"And the funny thing is that not only will a deep commitment to self-renewal and personal development make you a more effective parent, it will also make you a far happier person. As John F. Kennedy once said: 'Happiness is the fullest use of one's powers along lines of excellence.'"

"Okay, Julian, so what kinds of things can I do to renew myself and grow into a better, wiser and more complete human being?"

"One key is to start early," came the swift reply.

"Please explain."

"If you want to become a better person, I suggest you start by joining the Five o'clock Club, just like you did today."

"You want me to get up at 5 A.M. every day of the week?" I exclaimed. "Are you crazy?"

"The sages rose at 4 A.M., but 5 will do just fine for you, Catherine. By winning the battle of the bed, by putting mind over mattress and getting up early, you will get far more living out of life. Getting up at five will give you a psychological edge. The rest of the world is sleeping while you are up, doing all those things that the rest of humanity knows are important to do for a great life but never has the time to do."

"Like what?"

"Like watching the sun come up. Like walking in the woods. Like reading from the great books. As I mentioned to you earlier, reading a little bit each day will change your life. Reading inspiring, uplifting books for perhaps thirty minutes at the beginning of your day will infuse every remaining minute of your day with all the wisdom you connected with while others slept. It will improve the way you interact with the children. It will improve the way you interact with Jon. It will improve your relations with your employees. It will even make you kinder to complete strangers. As Judah ibn-Tibbon observed so sagely: 'Make thy books thy companions. Let thy cases and shelves be thy pleasure grounds and gardens.'"

"Powerful statement."

"Imagine having an extra hour or two every single morning for the rest of your life. Reserve that time for your inner work and watch your life soar to a completely new level. Use the time to meditate or visualize your ideal day or even your ideal life. Listen to lovely music to soothe your soul or spend the time cultivating a garden and communing with nature like our dear old friend Miss Williamson. As a matter of fact, she told me yesterday that she has woken up at 5 A.M. every day for over seventy years and it's the single best habit she has developed in her life."

"I didn't know that."

"Catherine, everyone on this planet—and I mean everyone—has a story to tell and a lesson to teach. The problem is that most of us are so busy—and so full of our own 'stuff' that we don't take the time to learn from those around us. I'm not faulting you, little sister. You have a busy career and a lovely family that demand your attention. I'm just reminding you to remember that a great life is made up of great relationships. If you want to be happier in life, get more connected to the people around you and watch the joy you feel grow. *Fulfillment in life does not come from collecting more things. It comes from feeling more love.*"

"I agree totally, Julian. These past few months have been the best times of my life. I've never been closer to Porter and Sarita. I've never felt more loved by Jon. I've never felt so appreciated by my staff. And I've never been so grateful for you. I've got a long way to go, but I know I'm headed in the right direction."

"No doubt about it. You are."

"So what else can I do to renew myself so I can grow into a better person?"

"Care for the temple," came Julian's reply.

"The 'temple' being?" I wondered aloud.

"Your body is your temple," Julian replied, removing the last vestiges of his scarecrow outfit to reveal the elegant robe that was now his trademark. "The ancient philosophers had a saying: 'Mens sana in corpore sano.'"

"Do translate. My Latin is not what it used to be," I said with a wink.

"It simply means that in a sound body rests a sound mind. This is such an incredibly important point of wisdom, and yet most people neglect it. Your body truly is your temple. You should come to see it as a vehicle that, when properly honored and cared for, will lead you to the greatest heights of your life. Striving for physical mastery is an excellent way to arrive at personal mastery."

"Really?"

"Sure. Think about all the discipline it takes to get into the gym five or six times a week. Think about how hard it is to keep stretching beyond our comfort zones in terms of the levels at which we exercise, and how challenging we find the thought of working out a little harder at every session. Think about the self-resolve required to eat healthy, natural foods and drink lots of water every day when every place we go seems to offer us other temptations. But if you have the courage to respect your body—the temple that houses the person that you are—personal mastery will not be far away. Each time you get into the gym for a workout on a day you just don't feel like exercising, you grow a little stronger as a human being. Each time you go out for a run on a cold winter's day when under the covers feels like the best place to be, you actualize your humanity just a little more. Working on improving your physical condition is a great way to improve your character and enrich the quality of your life. And not only will you improve as a person, you will improve as a parent."

"I'm not sure if I see the connection, big brother."

"Exercising regularly, eating well, and taking time to relax and nourish your body will make you feel happier. It will provide you with more energy than you have ever known. It will give you greater stamina and mental toughness. It will make you more patient and loving. And you will feel more serene during the hours of your days. Wouldn't these benefits help you to be a better parent for Porter and Sarita?" Julian asked rhetorically.

"Absolutely."

"Caring for the gift that is your body will even make you a clearer, stronger thinker. And since your thoughts ultimately form your world, that benefit alone is priceless. There are 168 hours in a week. Surely each and every one of us can carve out four or five of them to care for our temples and work on mastering our physical state, even within our hectic schedules. I know you've been exercising recently and I congratulate you on your progress, but I suggest that you take it to the next level. Get even more serious about liberating your physical potential and getting into the best possible condition."

"But let me ask you, Julian—isn't an obsessive focus on making our bodies perfect unhealthy? I feel so much pressure as a woman to look a certain way, especially given the media images we are surrounded by."

"Good point. Here's the key: I'm not suggesting that one's goal in striving for physical mastery is to look more like a supermodel or a movie star. The entire purpose of the pursuit is to discover *your best you*. And arriving at that point requires you to shift from an external focus to an internal one. Stop judging your physical progress against the women you see in the fashion magazines, and start measuring yourself against your previous self."

"That's a profound concept, Julian. I actually felt a tingle run down my spine when you said that."

"The great sages taught me that one. Remember the ancient Indian proverb that I told you about earlier? It said: 'There is nothing noble in being superior to others. True nobility lies in being superior to your former self.'"

"I remember it—and I love it!" I exclaimed. "That's a far more sensible—and enlightened—approach."

"So use your past self as your benchmark. And also remember that *the person who does not make time for exercise must eventually make time for illness.*"

"True," I said reflectively.

"It never ceases to amaze me," Julian continued with enormous enthusiasm, "how when we are young, we are willing to sacrifice all of our health for a little bit of wealth, and when we grow old and wise, we would be willing to sacrifice all of our wealth—"

"For a little bit of health," I interjected.

"Exactly. And by the way, when it comes to staying in peak shape and exercising to stay fit, please remember that every time you don't do the right thing, you fuel the habit of doing the wrong thing."

"You lost me again."

"Well, let me put it this way: a missed workout is much more than a missed workout."

"C'mon, Julian, quit fooling around," I stated.

"Okay. All I'm saying is that when you miss a workout, it's not like you just stay at the same level you were at— you actually take a few steps back. Every time you miss a workout, you have done something to strengthen the habit of not working out. And the more workouts you miss, the stronger that negative habit grows. Miss enough workouts, and eventually that negative habit of not working out will replace the positive habit of exercising that you have worked so very hard to cultivate. So that's why I say that every time you fail to do the right thing, you fuel the habit of doing the wrong thing. And this little principle applies throughout your life. Every time you forget to say thank you to someone, you have actually taken action to build the habit of never saying thank you. Every time you forget to return a phone call promptly, you have taken a step to develop the habit of never returning phone calls on time. Every time you tell your children you are too tired to read them a book at bedtime, you have done something to build the habit of never reading to them before they sleep. *Remember, Catherine, in life, the little things are actually the big things. And the quality of success you will experience in your life ultimately depends upon the tiny choices you make every minute of every hour of every day.*"

"I agree, Julian, it's so easy to forget that small daily acts define how big we end up living," I added, realizing that I was beginning to sound more and more like Julian as the days went by. "I guess that with the busy lives most of us lead, we just lose sight of The Things That Truly Count and end up focusing on the distractions. It brings to mind the words of management guru Peter Drucker. He said, 'There is nothing so useless as doing efficiently that which should not be done at all.'"

Julian began to laugh. "That's brilliant. I'll have to remember that one for sure. There's such truth in that statement. It truly makes no sense to spend the most important hours of your days doing the least important things. Wise leaders—and remember, we are all leaders of one sort or another—spend their days concentrating on what is worthy and essential in life. They take the time to figure out what their highest-leverage activities are—those actions that will yield the highest return on investment—and then they devote their energies only to those things. This heightened level of concentration around real priorities is the secret of success. As the Chinese mystic Lin Yutang observed: 'Besides the noble art of getting things done, master the noble art of leaving things undone. The wisdom of life consists in the elimination of nonessentials.'"

"What else can I do to renew myself and lead from within, Julian? Getting up early and caring for the temple are such excellent suggestions. I'd love to learn more."

"Recording your life is the next idea I have to offer for self-mastery."

"Here we go again! Okay, Julian," I remarked, playing along. "What does 'recording your life' mean?"

"I'm encouraging you to begin keeping a journal. In doing so, you will be in a position to learn from the significant events of your life and grow wiser with each passing day. Keeping a journal allows you to let your past serve you. It provides you with a tool that will help you leverage past experiences into future successes. Writing down the events of your days, along with the lessons you have drawn from them, will give you greater self-awareness. This will allow you greater clarity about why you do the things you do and what aspects of your actions need to be changed if you hope to evolve to the next stage of living. Writing in a journal offers you the opportunity to have regular one-on-one conversations with yourself. This discipline forces you to do some deep thinking in a world where deep thinking and introspection are undervalued. It will also help you live in a more conscious and intentional way, so that you act on life as opposed to life directing you."

"Journaling is that powerful a technique?"

"It is," replied Julian, biting into a huge, ripe tomato from Miss Williamson's garden.

"Shouldn't you wash that, Julian?" I wondered.

"You worry too much, Catherine. I'll be fine. Oh, in addition, a journal will provide you with a central place to record key insights on important issues, note key success strategies that you have learned from others or from observation and commit to all those things that you know are essential to achieving the high-quality personal, professional and spiritual life that you deserve."

"Can you elaborate on what you mean by 'spritual life'?"

"Sure. Actually, there's been a lot of confusion about the term these days. I'll just quote the Dalai Lama who said: 'When I use the word *spiritual*, I mean basic human good qualities. These are: human affection, a sense of involvement, honesty, discipline, and human intelligence properly guided by good motivation.' See, Catherine, these are the qualities that make us human beings. And we are all born with them at birth."

"We are?"

"Yup. We are all born as essentially spiritual beings—perfect in our imperfection. Unfortunately, as we grow, we tend to absorb negative patterns—those of our parents and then of our teachers and then of all those around us. Most people move farther and farther away from their authentic selves—the beings that they truly are—as they get older and more jaded by the world they perceive. My goal is to return to my essence and rediscover who I really am. To get back to the perfection that I once possessed before I allowed so much negativity to cloud the lens through which I see the universe."

"Wow. You really make me think, Julian. Now getting back to the process of journaling, is a journal a diary?"

"Another excellent question. No, a diary is a place where you record events, while a journal is a place where you analyze and evaluate them."

"Nice insight," I applauded.

"Keeping a journal encourages you to consider what you do, why you do it and what you have learned from all that you have done. Medical researchers have even found that writing in a private journal for as little as fifteen minutes a day can improve your health, the functioning of your immune system and your overall attitude. Remember, little sister, if your life is worth thinking about—and it is—it is worth writing about."

"Lovely advice."

"Which brings me to my final recommendation for self-renewal and personal mastery: take a weekly sabbatical."

"Sabbaticals are becoming popular in the business world these days. One of our managers just submitted a proposal to me in which he requests a year off to sail around the world with his family. He said he does not know who his kids are anymore and has lost his connection with his wife. Guess what my answer will be?" I smiled.

"I know. Good for you. But the kind of sabbatical that I am proposing to you is far less dramatic, but can be equally effective. In the ancient world, the seventh day of the week was called the Sabbath. It was reserved for some of life's important but commonly neglected pursuits, including spending time with one's family and pursuing one's passions. The Sabbath Day provided an opportunity for hard-working people to recharge their batteries and spend a day living life more fully. As the pace of life has quickened, however, this wonderful tradition has been lost along with the tremendous personal benefits that flowed from it. I'm encouraging you to restore this ritual for your own life. Set aside six or seven hours a week to enjoy the things you love to do but never get around to doing. You might do it on the weekend or, with your flexible schedule, your sabbatical might take place on a Tuesday or a Thursday. The point is to make sure that not even one week slips by when you don't take some time to show some loving kindness to yourself."

"Two questions immediately come to my mind. First, should I be alone during this weekly sabbatical; and second, what kinds of things should I be doing?"

"Yes, definitely do this alone. This is your opportunity to think and to really *be*. It's your chance to go for a solitary walk in the woods and feel the wind brush against your face. It's your chance to stop and listen to a street musician and not worry about rushing off to your next meeting. It's your chance to get lost in the shelves of your favorite bookstore while sipping on a cup of hot chocolate. It's your chance to dance in a park with no shoes on or to stare at a spider's web after it has rained—fully attentive and fully present. Really, it's a splendid opportunity to be completely alive, each and every week for the rest of your life."

"So a weekly sabbatical is a gift I give to myself," I offered.

"Excellent point. It truly is. It's your reward for a week well spent. And it will undoubtedly have the effect of keeping you happy, fresh, energized, relaxed, and playful. It is an excellent use of your time, an investment that will allow you to perform at your best through the week as a parent, partner, and person."

"You know, this habit will work wonders for me, I just know it. It will give me a little breathing space. I think I'll begin this Friday. The morning will start with a massage. Then I'll write in my journal in some natural place. And I'll cap the morning off with a vegetarian lunch at the new restaurant by the river."

"Food's excellent there," Julian piped up. "The owner used to be a client of mine. He treats me like a prince every time I go there and loads up on the garlic, just the way I like it. Umm, umm—garlic power! Lucky I don't have to share my room with anyone after those feasts," he chuckled happily.

"You're too much, Julian. I had no idea that's where you've been disappearing to these days. You sometimes vanish for hours and hours," I continued cautiously. "Sometimes we hear this sawing noise coming from your room. Other times we hear hammering. At other times, I hear you leaving in the middle of the night. I want you to have your independence, but I must confess that I really do worry about you."

"Thanks for the concern, Catherine. I've got things to do and people to meet," came the only reply I could elicit.

"Okay, back to this beautiful idea of taking a sabbatical each and every week to restore myself. Any other things I should know about it?"

"Well, I think you are on the right track. Use it as a time to play, to dance, to think, to nourish your spirit, and to awaken to the wonders of life. It's also a great chance to develop your attitude of gratitude. Take some time every week and list all the blessings in your life in your journal. Remember, what you focus on grows, what you think about expands, and what you dwell on determines your destiny. The aspects of your life that you devote the most attention to are the ones that you will see blossom into even greater marvels. So stay centered on all the good in your life, and you'll find it will grow.

Suffering in life is really nothing more than the difference between the way things are and the way you imagine they should be. If you can come to accept the blessings of your present reality without always feeling that your life is hollow as compared to the lives of others, you will have taken a quantum leap toward enlightenment. Really commit to becoming a person who lives life in a constant state of gratitude and positive expectation. Dream big dreams, but also savor the place where you find yourself to be at any time. The road really is as good as the end. When you can maintain this frame of mind, the universe will be sure to shower its abundance on you. I love the words of Cicero, who noted: 'Gratitude is not only the greatest of virtues, but the mother of all the rest.'"

Julian then began to walk into the center of the garden, his arms outstretched as if he were expecting a gift from the heavens for all the wisdom and love he had shared with me. Just as his arms reached higher, a burst of light seemed to streak across the sky. "Did you see that?" he exclaimed, his face completely animated and his eyes wide as ever.

"Unbelievable. What was that?"

"I'm not sure," replied Julian. "But it does help me make a point that I've been hoping to share with you all morning, Catherine."

"Which is?"

"Be a light. Be a light to your children and show them the way. Be a light to Jon and illuminate his life. And be a light in this world so it becomes a better, wiser, more peaceful place to be. You are such an extraordinary woman. Please take the lessons I have given you and use them to grow into the person that I know, deep in my heart, you were meant to be. In everything you do, from now on, show up at your best and play full out. Be a light where there is darkness. Be a guide when others are lost. And never forget that a loving heart and a rich spirit will improve the planet in ways you cannot even begin to imagine."

With that, Julian reached down and began to place his hands in the soil, digging down. He dug deeper and deeper, the expression on his face revealing the single-minded focus that had been one of the keys to the amazing success he had experienced over the course of his lifetime.

After a few minutes of feverish activity, Julian stopped. Sweat beaded on his brow, and his robe was flecked with sprinkles of dirt. Julian quickly reached into the hole he'd been digging and pulled out an object the likes of which I'd never seen before. It was about five inches long, appeared to be made from stone, and resembled a human being standing with hands outstretched.

"What's that?" I asked with a pounding heart.

"It's called an Inukshuk. They originated in the Arctic, one of the least populated places on the planet, but one that offers us many lessons about how the community of humanity needs to start living. According to Inuit legend, the Inukshuk is a guide for a safe journey through the travels of our lives and symbolizes the duty of each and every one of us to light up the path of those who may have lost their way. For centuries, these stone figures, shaped in human form, have guided travelers through the desolate lands of the Arctic and have comforted those in need of direction. You, my dear sister, are growing into a light—a guide of sorts—who will lead your family, as well as all the other people whose lives you will touch, into a much wiser way of living. I knew such a day would eventually come. And so while my eyes were being opened to a whole new reality in India, I arranged for this gift to be placed here for you. All that time, I didn't know exactly when I would present it to you or whether it would even be here. But I trusted my heart and found it, exactly where I was told it would be."

As I reached over and grasped the Inukshuk from Julian's open hands, I saw four words scrawled on its stone surface. They read simply: "Pay Attention to Life." It made me think of the words of Henry Miller that Julian had written in huge letters on the center of his ceiling:

The moment one gives close attention to anything, even a blade of grass, it becomes a mysterious, awesome, indescribably magnificent world in itself.

The Fifth Mastery of the Family Leader™

Give Your Child Immortality Through the
Gift of a Legacy

*"Few will have the greatness to bend history
itself, but each one of us can work to change a
small portion of events, and in the total of all
those acts will be written the history of this
generation."*
—Robert F. Kennedy

*"There comes a special moment in everyone's
life, a moment for which that person was born.
That special opportunity, when he seizes it,
will fulfill his mission—a mission for which
he is uniquely qualified. In that moment, he
finds his greatness. It is his finest hour."*
—Winston Churchill

I HADN'T BEEN TO THE OXFORD MOVIE HALL IN years. In its heyday, it was known as the hippest place in the city to see films, rub shoulders with the stars, and spend a memorable Saturday night. But the fast crowd had moved on to other venues, and the owners had let the Oxford run down. Although movies still played there, they were never the big releases, and the theater always remained half full at best.

It was a Tuesday night, and Julian had asked me to meet him there for the seven o'clock showing of a documentary about a woman named Oseola McCarty that was called *The Washerwoman Who Touched the World*. I knew nothing about the documentary, or about the woman who was its subject, but Julian said it was important that I learn more about her life, and I relished the thought of watching the movie with my brother.

The six weeks that had passed since I learned of the Fourth Mastery of the Family Leader in Miss Williamson's back garden had seen changes in my life that could best be described as miraculous. I had taken Julian's advice and was well on my way to becoming a lifetime member of The Five o'clock Club. At first I wasn't at all sure that I had it in me to get up at that time every morning, but after surviving the first few painful weeks, the habit fit like a glove. In the extra hours I gained by getting up early, I would commune with nature, meditate, and read through the books of philosophy that Julian had been leaving on the coffee table in our living room. Or I would use the time to plan out my days, strategize about my life, and further define my dreams. Many mornings, I would simply sit in our uncluttered den and stare out the window at the huge rose garden that Jon and I loved so much, savoring the silence and basking in tranquility. Those times of solitude brought deep insights on how I was to live out the rest of my days and the value that I could add to the world if I truly became the leader that my family deserved. The French philosopher Blaise Pascal was so right when he said, "All man's miseries derive from not being able to sit quietly in a room alone."

I rose to higher levels of thinking and being over those six weeks, experiencing new thoughts and feelings I never thought I owned. I came to see the world as a better and happier place and finally felt that my role within it was a significant one. I gave more love to the kids and Jon than I'd ever been able to give in the past and, in turn, I received more love from them than I ever thought possible. The darkness that had always seemed to engulf my heart slowly subsided, and I began to detect a sense of wonder in everything around me. Julian had said this would happen. And it did.

Taking Julian's advice about caring for the temple made a profound improvement in my energy level and vastly improved my moods as well. I felt able to do more with Jon and the children and enjoy more time with myself. Keeping a journal helped heighten my awareness of how I was living each day and conduct each one that followed more wisely. And the weekly sabbatical concept reconnected me to my inner sense of spirit and joy—something that I had lost so many years ago. I began to feel I was "letting my bigness" shine through, as Julian would say, and liberating my best self in the process. And as my brother promised, becoming a better person most certainly made me a better parent.

But I must also confess that I had begun to feel a little sad. Though he never came right out and said it, I got the feeling that Julian was planning to leave us. One evening, as we all sat down for our family meal, he asked Jon how long it would take for a person to get to Mexico by bus. Another night he asked Porter to print out a map of Canada off the Internet. And on another occasion, Julian received a FedEx package marked with the message "Enclosed please find your information package on Italy." I guess I knew in my heart that Julian had come to teach me the lessons I most needed to learn in my life and that once I had learned them, he would be off to find his next project. But my mind just couldn't accept the fact that I might have to live the rest of my life without the enlightened presence of the brother whom I loved so much.

Adding to my unease were the strange noises that continued to emanate from Julian's room above the garage. The hammering, sawing, and sanding sometimes went on for hours on end, with Julian finally emerging with a huge smile on his face and sawdust dancing off his robe. He didn't tell me what he was up to, and I didn't ask him what was going on up there. Henry David Thoreau once wrote, "If a man does not keep pace with his companions, perhaps it is because he hears a different drummer. Let him step to the music which he hears, however measured and far away." Giving Julian his space was, for me, all about letting him step to his own music.

As I walked into the movie hall, I saw no sign of Julian. He had told me to sit in the seventh row and to save him a seat in case he arrived late. As the lights dimmed, an usher walked to the center of the room, and a spotlight illuminated his youthful face. He began to speak. "Good evening, ladies and gentlemen. Thanks for joining us here tonight at the Oxford for the evening showing of a new documentary about a very special woman. Please turn your cellphones off and enjoy the show." The theater was now completely dark, and the film's opening music started to play. Just then, I felt a tap on my arm. I looked up and saw Julian carrying two large bags of popcorn, two big bottles of spring water, and a bag of jellybeans. On his back was a knapsack that drew creases across the front of his robe.

"Sorry I'm late, little sister. I was cleaning a few things up at home," he offered with a grand smile.

"No problem, Julian. I was beginning to think I would be stood up tonight, though," I laughed as he sat down and passed me my portion of the goodies.

"Not a chance, Catherine. I've been looking forward to tonight all week. This is an amazing story," he replied, reaching over and planting a light kiss on my forehead.

The story of the life of Oseola McCarty was indeed amazing. Born into poverty, she grew up in a tiny house that she never left except to go up the street to buy groceries and to visit her church. She made her living washing other people's dirty laundry, carefully saving the nickels and the dimes and the quarters that were offered to her in return. She never learned how to drive and she never got married—although she did say to a reporter when she was in her late eighties that she was "still looking for a good man." Oseola lived a simple, decent, and frugal life, dutifully putting aside the money that she earned day after day, week after week, month after month as the decades slipped away.

One day, at the age of eighty-seven, she walked into her local bank and was greeted by a banker who asked her whether she had an idea how of much she had accumulated as a result of these small daily contributions she had been making over the course of her life. When she indicated that she had no idea, he smiled and informed her that over one-quarter of a million dollars sat in her bank account. Sensing that Oseola had no concept of how much money that was, the banker took out ten dimes and placed them on the counter. "These ten dimes represent your money, Oseola. What will you do with them?" She pointed to the first dime and vowed to give it to the church. The next three dimes were reserved for her much-loved nieces and nephews. And then a lovely smile came to Oseola's face as she said that the remaining dimes were to be used for something very special.

One month later, the local university in Oseola's hometown received a check from her for $150,000, with a request that it be used to set up a scholarship fund to help poor students fulfill their dreams. I learned from the documentary that this act of humanity touched people around the world. Oseola was honored by presidents and prime ministers and even received an honorary doctorate from Harvard University, Julian's alma mater. Through all the hoopla, she maintained that she still wanted to live out her life in a simple and principled way. But she did have one dream—to see the first recipient of the scholarship she had created grace the graduation stage. But she confided that she never expected that dream to be realized given her advanced age. One month before Oseola died, however, the first recipient of her scholarship walked across the platform to receive her reward.

After Oseola passed away, a reporter called that young scholarship winner and asked her for a comment on the death of her benefactor. The student offered this response: "Heaven couldn't have gotten a better angel.

She was an inspiration, a blessing, a treasure to the entire earth."

After the documentary ended and the crowd had left, Julian began to speak in the empty movie hall.

"'Mankind's common instinct for reality has always held the world to be essentially a theater for heroism,'" were his first words, quoting William James, the brilliant early twentieth-century psychologist. "I brought you here to this old theater that our city has forgotten to make this essential point.

"Your life, Catherine, is ultimately a theater for heroism. The remaining days of your life—and there will be many—must become a stage for noble acts of leadership and kindness," spoke Julian with heated emotion. I dared not interject.

"Look at the life of Oseola McCarty," he continued. "She washed people's dirty clothes to make ends meet. She lived in a tiny home and was unknown to the world. And yet through her small daily acts of contribution— saving those coins over all those years for a worthy cause—she blessed the world. What a glorious legacy this woman left."

"Do we all have it within us to leave this kind of a legacy?" I asked softly.

"Absolutely. As a matter of fact, I learned from the sages that we are all programmed to do something special with our lives and live on in the hearts of others when we leave. The sad thing is that most of us think that, in order to leave a significant legacy, we must perform some truly great act. Only then, we feel, will our lives be validated and our highest duties fulfilled. But that's not what is required of most of us. All we need to do to leave a meaningful mark on the world is focus on performing small acts of greatness each and every day. When you do this, your legacy will take care of itself."

"Sort of how Oseola McCarty's small, daily—seemingly insignificant—acts of depositing those coins into her account added up to something huge at the end of her life?" I asked.

"Exactly," replied Julian with a satisfied look. "Do the little things with great love and attention and the big things will take care of themselves. And that's really what the Fifth and final Mastery of the Family Leader is all about: *Give Your Child Immortality Through the Gift of a Legacy.*"

"Wow, that one sounds incredible," I said with a mix of excitement and sadness—this was the final lesson I was to learn from Julian.

"It is the most important mastery of all, Catherine. It's the one that requires you to teach Porter and Sarita that at the end of the day, their destiny as people is to live for something more important than themselves. And if they accept this challenge, as I know they will, they will achieve immortality in the sense that they will live on in the hearts of those whose lives they have touched."

Just then the words "Destiny Pictures" flashed across the movie screen. "Did you arrange that, Julian?"

"No," he responded, "but it does speak to my point. You see, we all have a vital destiny that we are duty bound to follow if we hope to live our highest lives. Think of what Vaclav Havel said: 'The real test of a man is not when he plays the role he wants for himself, but when he plays the role destiny has for him.'"

"And what can I do to help Porter and Sarita discover this 'vital destiny'?"

"Easy," replied Julian. "Coach them to listen to the gentle whispers of the holiest places of their hearts."

"Please do explain," I requested, as a cleaner walked in and began mopping up the floor.

"Good evening, Mr. Mantle," he said.

"Julian, does everyone know you?" I asked in wonder. "I mean, how would even the night cleaner of this particular theater know you?"

"Because I've been here to see this documentary about ten times over the past few weeks," he replied with a laugh. "Oseola's story is a good lesson for me. It reminds me of the importance of contribution, of making my life even more valuable by living it for others—by giving it over to the benefit of the world. Anyway, to answer your question, listening to the gentle whispers of the holiest places of the heart is all about discovering—and then heeding—the calls that come from the deepest place within you. Sometimes we hear these whispers when we are completely connected with nature, while we are out for a solitary walk in the woods on a magnificent autumn day, for example. Sometimes we hear these whispers while we are experiencing silence—in meditation or another form of contemplation. And sometimes these calls come to us in life's most trying and seemingly hopeless moments, like when someone we love dies or when one of our dreams shatters. The point of wisdom is simply this: pay attention and be aware of the inner voices that will lead you down the path of your destiny. Listen to what your heart tells you to do. And commit yourself to living out your destiny so you will leave a meaningful legacy."

"I'm not sure if I know how I can teach this to the kids at the age they're at," I confided.

"You are the best judge of that, Catherine. Yes, they are young, but you just might find that it's an ideal time to give them an appreciation of the importance of listening to their hearts as well as living in a way that is helpful to other people. At least give them an understanding of the importance of enjoying silent moments. As they get older, let them know that no matter what they decide to do for a living, they will receive your unconditional love and support. Share with them how essential a regular period of soul searching is for their continued evolution. Inspire them to dream greatly and to see that success in life comes from living in a significant way— that is, a way that contributes to the world in some measure. A superb question that you should encourage them to ask themselves over and over is simply: 'How can I be most useful and valuable to the world?' Another excellent question is 'What is the highest use of my time and talents?' Kierkegaard once observed that the main responsibility of a human being is to 'find an idea for which they can live and die.' I'd have to agree. To discover a compelling cause that you would be willing to die for, some aim that can help even one life improve and that fires up your soul, is to begin to truly live. And at that moment, the entire universe becomes an agent for your success."

"Really?"

"Most certainly," replied Julian with complete confidence. "The universe has a grand plan for each and every one of us. Once you figure out what the plan is and take steps to align yourself with it, sparks start to fly. So my final lesson to you is that you teach those lovely, intelligent, wonderful kids of yours that greatness as a human being comes from beginning something in their lives that does not end with them."

"You're talking about starting something that lives on after their lives end? A legacy?"

"Yes. See, the deepest need of the human heart is the need to live for something more important than ourselves. If Porter and Sarita get that point—if nothing else—they will succeed in a way that will astonish you. I'm talking about success in the truest sense. Success that goes far beyond having a nice BMW parked in the driveway or beautiful suits to wear to work. I'm talking about the kind of success that fills the world with light and with greater love. I'm talking about the kind of success that makes people want to be more and do more for others. I'm speaking of the kind of success that would make you the proudest parent on the planet."

"I'm speechless," I said, as tears welled up in my eyes.

"Each and every one of us needs to ask ourselves, not just as parents but as people, 'What will my life stand for after I have died?' We need to think about the footprints we will leave and how future generations will know that we have lived. I'm not saying we all have to be Gandhis or Mother Teresas. Those were the paths that were mapped out for those people. What I am saying is that we all need to conduct our lives in a way that will transcend ourselves. We need to avoid being shallow and complaining that the world will not take care of us. Instead, we need to take care of our world and live out our days in a way that shows compassion, concern, and care for others. We need to let go of the shackles that keep our thoughts restrained and our actions small, and dare to see what our best selves really look like. To do this, Catherine, to be this, is to truly live. Give the gift of this wisdom to your children and you will be doing a noble deed as a parent. Govern your life by it and you will ensure that you will always be a great person."

"Thanks, Julian," I replied lovingly, as Julian reached over and gave me a tender hug that filled me with warmth and deep emotion.

"Catherine."

"Yes," I responded, fearing the worst.

"Tonight is my last night with you. I've said goodbye to Jon and the children, and now I must do the same with you. This is the most difficult parting of my life. I so dearly wish I could live with you until I die, but that is not what I have been called to do. I promised the Great Sages of Sivana that I would spread the wisdom they so generously shared with me with those who need to hear it, and that is the work I must continue to do. I love you so very much, and am so proud of the things you have been doing, as well as the woman that you have become. You have embraced The Five Masteries with open arms and are leading your family to a place of greatness. You have grown into a wise guide and a powerful light that will lead your loved ones and others in your life to an understanding of what we are all meant to do while we reside in the world."

Julian then closed his eyes and clasped his hands together in the traditional Indian way. "I honor the best within you, little sister. I will always be with you as you journey along life's road. I will always be near you as you overcome life's challenges. And I will always be sending you the purest love of a brother as you share yours with your family." After a long pause he added: "May the saddest days of your future be far far happier than the happiest days of your past, little sister. I love you."

And with that, Julian kissed me gently on my forehead, brushed the fallen morsels of popcorn off his robe and ran out of the theater, where I had learned what heroism in this gift we call life is all about.

I sat in my seat for what seemed to be an eternity, my heart filled with sadness at the loss that I felt. Finally, I stood up and prepared to leave. Jon would be wondering where I was, and I still had to make the children's lunches for school the next day. As I moved toward the door, something fell off the seat that Julian had been sitting on and fell to the floor with a clank. I picked it up and carried it out of the theater into the street, where I was greeted by the shining beams of a strikingly beautiful harvest moon.

It was the key to Julian's room above the garage. A typed label had been attached to it reading: *The key to wisdom lies within your own home*. I wasn't sure what Julian was referring to, but I placed the key in my purse, wiped away the tears that had continued to fall and made my way to my family. On a hunch, I decided to go up to Julian's room before going inside our house. I walked up the steps and inserted the key into the lock. He had left the lights on for me. As I walked into the small but impeccably kept room, I was astonished by what I saw.

The entire room had been transformed into a magnificent library, with ornately bound books lining the most beautiful shelves I had ever seen. The smell of sandal-wood wafted through the air and a feeling of deep peace pulsed through my body. I looked at the books, which bore names like *A Manual for Living* by Epictetus, *The Meditations of Marcus Aurelius* and *Letters from a Stoic* by Seneca. The collection had been lovingly treated and organized with immense care.

I then found a note from Julian. It read:

Words cannot express my love for you, Porter, Sarita, and Jon so I will not even try to do so. Instead, my dear sister Catherine, I will give you the greatest gift I know of—the gift of wisdom. This library, containing some of the most important books ever written, is for Porter and Sarita. It is my great hope that you and Jon will share many happy moments and many great times up here with these two very special children. And as you all learn from the pages of these extraordinary books, perhaps you will think of me.

The note was signed "In leadership and in love, your brother Julian."

As I walked out of our new library and down the recently painted steps, my heart danced with joy. I felt exhilarated and excited by the promise of our family's future. I felt wiser, happier, and more enlightened than ever before. As I entered my home, I paused to enjoy the song that gently flowed out of the open window of

Julian's room—he had left the CD player running. The words I heard—"What a wonderful world"—began to make me cry. Then they made me smile.

THE SHARMA LIFE
LEADERSHIP REPORT™

FREE subscription offer to purchasers of *Family Wisdom from The Monk Who Sold His Ferrari* for a limited time only. (Annual subscription has a $95 value.)

The Sharma Life Leadership Report, Robin Sharma's hugely popular electronic newsletter, is packed with practical wisdom, lessons, and tips that you can apply immediately to improve the quality of your life. This highly inspirational report focuses on leading-edge topics for personal, professional, and character development including self-esteem, inner renewal, peak performance, discipline, creativity, life-career balance, relationships, self-leadership, stress mastery, and career leadership. Join the thousands who love this extraordinary learning tool!

To order your free subscription, simply visit **www.robinsharma.com** and register on-line today.

KEYNOTES & SEMINARS WITH ROBIN SHARMA

#1 Bestselling Author & Professional Speaker

Robin Sharma is one of the world's most thought-provoking and electrifying professional speakers. His powerful wisdom and pioneering insights on leadership, managing rapid change, personal effectiveness, and life renewal have made him the first choice of organizations seeking a high-profile keynote speaker or seminar leader whose message will transform lives and restore commitment in these turbulent times. Robin Sharma's enormously inspirational presentations are fully customized through a unique research process, rich in practical content and designed to help your people rise to all-new levels of performance, passion, creativity, and personal fulfillment. Recent clients include Microsoft, FedEx, Kraft, IBM, and General Motors.

To book Robin for your next conference or in-house seminar, visit **www.robinsharma.com** or call:

Marnie Ballane
V.P. Speaking Services
Sharma Leadership International
Telephone: 1-888-RSHARMA (774-2762)
E-mail: marnie@robinsharma.com

PERSONAL COACHING
WITH ROBIN SHARMA

1. THE MONTHLY COACH ™

The Monthly Coach is Robin's highly acclaimed book- and CD-of-the-month club. Each month, you receive one of the most powerful books available on personal development and self-discovery, along with a CD recording of Robin's summary of the book's best points and his insights on how to translate the book's knowledge into real results in your life. This program is life changing.

2. THE ROBIN SHARMA LIFE COACHING PROCESS ™

This is Robin's revolutionary system for people who are ready to create extraordinary lives. You meet with Robin in a small group setting every month over the course of six months to experience one of the most effective programs for personal transformation and self-renewal available today. Open to participants across the U.S. and Canada.

3. THE ELITE PERFORMERS SERIES ™: Corporate Coaching

The Elite Performers Series is Sharma Leadership International's flagship corporate coaching program, which is designed to transform employees into high performers who excel amid change. Presented by Robin to your organization's employees, over two incredible days, The Elite Performers Series will inspire your team to operate at all-new levels of effectiveness, excellence, and personal responsibility. This is one of the best leadership training programs available today.

4. THE MASTERS SERIES

This is an exclusive program for top executives and entrepreneurs seeking world-class, one-on-one coaching to create extraordinary results both professionally and personally. You meet weekly with one of our Lead Coaches via telephone or the Internet and experience a powerful process that has helped thousands of people transform the way they think, feel, and act. Robin Sharma himself accepts up to five executive coaching clients each year to serve as their personal life coach. The results are always the same: complete life transformation.

For more information on these personal coaching options, please visit **robinsharma.com** for full details or contact Al Moscardelli, at:

Sharma Leadership International
Toll-free: 1-888-RSHARMA (774-2762)
e-mail: coaching@robinsharma.com
Website: **www.robinsharma.com**

POWERFUL WISDOM FOR LEADERSHIP
IN BUSINESS AND IN LIFE

NOW AVAILABLE IN ALL GOOD BOOKSTORES

Discounts available on quantity purchases for your
organization. Please call 1-888-RSHARMA
or e-mail info@robinsharma.com for pricing information.

WE HAVE A REQUEST

Robin Sharma would love to hear how this book has affected both you and your organization. Share your success stories, insights, and experiences. Do you have a tip or quotes that you would like to share with other readers in Robin's popular newsletter, *The Sharma Life Leadership Report*™? Please send them to us. Robin will make every possible effort to respond with a personal note. We want to hear from you!

Please connect with Robin by sending him an e-mail. His direct address is: **wisdom@robinsharma.com**. You can also mail him a letter c/o:

Sharma Leadership International
304 Newbury Street, #519
Boston, MA 02115-2832
Toll-free: 1-888-RSHARMA (774-2762)
Website: **www.robinsharma.com**

For Robin's latest thinking on personal leadership and life management, visit **www.robinsharma.com**, one of the Internet's most popular destinations for personal success and professional mastery.

About the Author

ROBIN SHARMA is one of the world's premier thinkers on leadership in business and success in life. He is the author of numerous books, including the #1 international bestseller *The Monk Who Sold His Ferrari*; its bestselling sequel *Leadership Wisdom from The Monk Who Sold His Ferrari*; and *Who Will Cry When You Die?* and *The Saint, the Surfer, and the CEO*. Sharma is also in constant demand across the globe as a keynote speaker for organizations dedicated to developing leaders at all levels and as an executive coach to people ready to create extraordinary work and personal lives. Clients include Fortune 500 companies such as Microsoft, General Motors, IBM, FedEx, as well as health-care firms and public-sector organizations.

A former lawyer who holds two law degrees, including a master's of law, Robin Sharma is the CEO of Sharma Leadership International (SLI), a widely respected training firm that offers a range of services and products to help employees realize their highest potential for exceptional professional and personal results amidst relentless change, including The Elite Performers Series™, the landmark two-day leadership transformation program. SLI also runs the highly acclaimed *Robin Sharma Life Coaching Program*™, a strikingly effective coaching process that shows individuals and corporate teams how to create the personal lives they want while becoming a star at work. In addition, Sharma Leadership International offers *The Monthly Coach* program—the acclaimed book/CD-of-the-month club where Robin personally selects a life changing work that will enhance your growth and enrich your life. He will send it to you every 30 days for continual improvement. For more information on any of these services or to see our complete line of learning products, please visit **www.robinsharma.com** or call **1-888-RSHARMA**.

Notes

Notes

Notes

Notes

We hope you enjoyed this Hay House book. If you would like to receive a free catalog featuring additional Hay House books and products, or if you would like information about the Hay Foundation, please contact:

Hay House, Inc.
P.O. Box 5100
Carlsbad, CA 92018-5100

(760) 431-7695 or (800) 654-5126
(760) 431-6948 (fax) or (800) 650-5115 (fax)
www.hayhouse.com

❧ ❧

Published and distributed in Australia by: Hay House Australia, Ltd. • 18/36 Ralph St. • Alexandria NSW 2015
Phone: 612-9669-4299 • *Fax:* 612-9669-4144 • www.hayhouse.com.au

Published and distributed in the United Kingdom by: Hay House UK, Ltd. • Unit 202, Canalot Studios
222 Kensal Rd., London W10 5BN • *Phone:* 44-20-8962-1230
Fax: 44-20-8962-1239 • www.hayhouse.co.uk

Published and distributed in the Republic of South Africa by: Hay House SA (Pty), Ltd., P.O. Box 990, Witkoppen 2068
Phone/Fax: 2711-7012233 • orders@psdprom.co.za

❧ ❧

Sign up via the Hay House USA Website to receive the Hay House online newsletter and stay informed about what's going on with your favorite authors. You'll receive bimonthly announcements about: Discounts and Offers, Special Events, Product Highlights, Free Excerpts, Giveaways, and more!